The 80/20 Principle

THE SECRET OF ACHIEVING MORE WITH LESS

from SmarterComics

Richard Koch

The 80/20 Principle

THE SECRET OF ACHIEVING MORE WITH LESS

from SmarterComics

Richard Koch

Chris Moreno	Illustrator
Cullen Bunn	Script
D.J. Kirbride	Editor
Jennifer Kunz	Creative Director
Sander Pieterse	Media Designer
Franco Arda	CEO SmarterComics

Printed in Canada

ISBN-13: 978-1-61082-000-4

The Graphic Novel version is published by arrangement with Nicholas Brealey Publishing, London. Copyright © 2007, 1997 by Richard Koch. This New Edition of 'THE 80/20 PRINCIPLE: The Secret of Achieving More with Less' published by Nicholas Brealey Publishing, London, 2007.

FOREWORD

Wow!

When I was contacted about a comic book version of my bestseller The 80/20 Principle, I instantly knew it was a great idea. But when they showed me samples of what it would look like, I was blown away!

This edition is so powerful visually, and yet so faithful to all the original ideas and insights, that it's like having a translation into a new and better language. On reflection, that's precisely what it is – a quicker, easier and funnier way to grasp the wonderful truth behind the 80/20 principle.

The principle says that most things we want, or want to avoid, flow from a very few causes. So if we know what they are, and how to tap into them, we can achieve much more of what makes us useful and happy with much less effort.

Then I realized – the comic book itself is a terrific manifestation of the 80/20 principle – it's more amusing and easier to read a comic, and we grasp the point so quickly, that the comic is a superior in many ways to pages of text. We think of comics as juvenile, but they may be the language of the angels.

So – that's a good reason to stop reading these words and get on with looking at the illustrations. They just might take your life to a level you never expected.

Enjoy the ride!

Richard Koch

Gibraltar, August 2011

"THE 80/20 PRINCIPLE IS THE CORNERSTONE OF RESULT BASED LIVING."

TIM FERRIS
AUTHOR OF THE 4-HOUR WORKWEEK

THE 80/20 PRINCIPLE CAN AND SHOULD BE USED BY EVERY INTELLIGENT PERSON IN HIS OR HER DAILY LIFE...
80
20
...BY EVERY ORGANIZATION, AND BY EVERY SOCIAL GROUPING AND FORM OF SOCIETY.

IT CAN HELP INDIVIDUALS AND GROUPS ACHIEVE MORE WITH MUCH LESS EFFORT.
THE 80/20 PRINCIPLE CAN RAISE PERSONAL EFFECTIVENESS AND HAPPINESS.

IT CAN MULTIPLY THE PROFITABILITY OF CORPORATIONS AND THE EFFECTIVENESS OF ANY ORGANIZATION.
IT EVEN HOLDS THE KEY TO RAISING THE QUALITY AND QUANTITY OF PUBLIC SERVICES WHILE CUTTING THEIR COSTS.

THE PRINCIPLE IS ONE OF THE BEST WAYS OF NOT ONLY DEALING WITH, BUT *TRANSCENDING* THE PRESSURES OF MODERN LIFE.

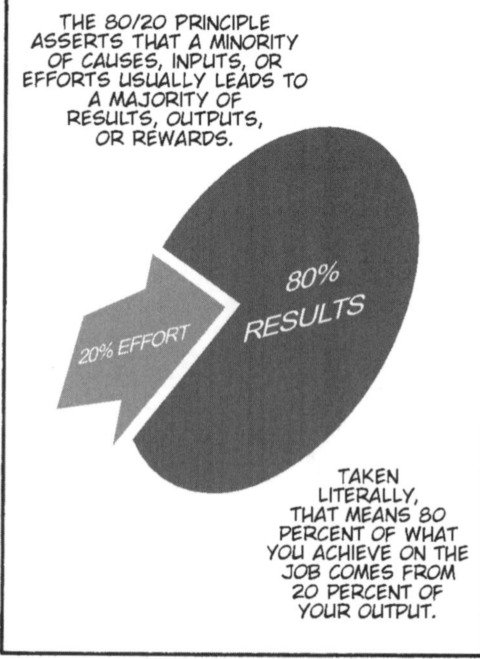
THE 80/20 PRINCIPLE ASSERTS THAT A MINORITY OF CAUSES, INPUTS, OR EFFORTS USUALLY LEADS TO A MAJORITY OF RESULTS, OUTPUTS, OR REWARDS.
20% EFFORT
80% RESULTS
TAKEN LITERALLY, THAT MEANS 80 PERCENT OF WHAT YOU ACHIEVE ON THE JOB COMES FROM 20 PERCENT OF YOUR OUTPUT.

THUS, THE DOMINANT PART OF YOUR OUTPUT IS LARGELY IRRELEVANT.
THIS IS CONTRARY TO WHAT MOST PEOPLE EXPECT.

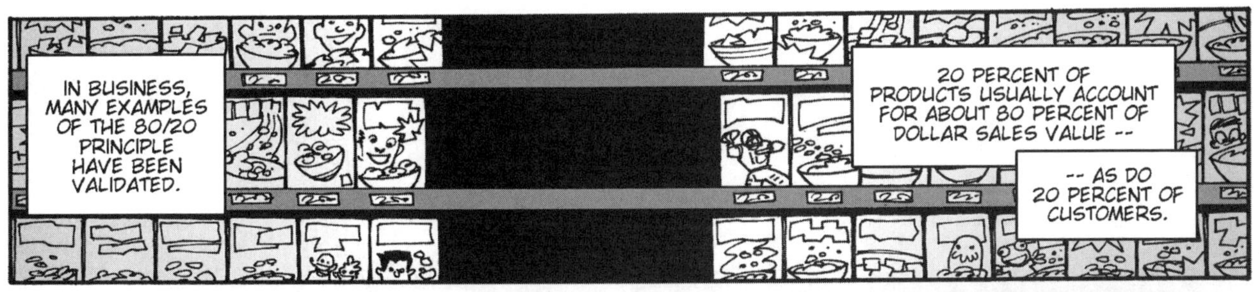
IN BUSINESS, MANY EXAMPLES OF THE 80/20 PRINCIPLE HAVE BEEN VALIDATED.
20 PERCENT OF PRODUCTS USUALLY ACCOUNT FOR ABOUT 80 PERCENT OF DOLLAR SALES VALUE --
-- AS DO 20 PERCENT OF CUSTOMERS.

IN SOCIETY, 20 PERCENT OF CRIMINALS ACCOUNT FOR 80 PERCENT OF ALL CRIME.

20 PERCENT OF MOTORISTS CAUSE 80 PERCENT OF ACCIDENTS.

20 PERCENT OF THOSE WHO MARRY COMPRISE 80 PERCENT OF DIVORCE RATES.

IN THE HOME, 20 PERCENT OF YOUR CARPETS ARE LIKELY TO GET 80 PERCENT OF THE WEAR.
20 PERCENT OF YOUR CLOTHES WILL BE WORN 80 PERCENT OF THE TIME.

THE INTERNAL COMBUSTION ENGINE IS A GREAT TRIBUTE TO THE 80/20 PRINCIPLE.
80 PERCENT OF THE ENERGY IS WASTED IN COMBUSTION, AND ONLY 20 PERCENT GETS TO THE WHEELS.
THIS 20 PERCENT OF THE INPUT GENERATES 100 PERCENT OF THE OUTPUT.

THE PATTERN UNDERLYING TO 80/20 PRINCIPLE WAS DISCOVERED IN 1897 BY ITALIAN ECONOMIST VILFREDO PARETO.

HE HAPPENED TO BE LOOKING AT PATTERNS OF WEALTH AND INCOME IN NINETEENTH-CENTURY ENGLAND.
HE FOUND THAT MOST INCOME AND WEALTH WENT TO A MINORITY OF PEOPLE IN HIS SAMPLES.

OVER A CENTURY AFTER PARETO, THE IMPLICATIONS OF THE 80/20 PRINCIPLE HAVE SURFACED IN CONTROVERSY OVER THE ASTRONOMIC AND EVER-INCREASING INCOMES GOING TO SUPERSTARS...
The highest paid actors
The Wealthiest People in the World
ENTERTAINMENT NATIO
Superstar Salaries Sky-rocket
Alison's
...AND THOSE VERY FEW PEOPLE AT THE TOP OF A GROWING NUMBER OF PROFESSIONS.

WHY SHOULD YOU CARE ABOUT THE 80/20 PRINCIPLE?
WHETHER YOU REALIZE IT OR NOT, THE PRINCIPLE APPLIES TO YOUR LIFE, TO YOUR SOCIAL WORLD, AND TO YOUR WORKPLACE.
UNDERSTANDING THE 80/20 PRINCIPLE GIVES YOU GREAT INSIGHT INTO THE WORLD AROUND YOU.

OUR DAILY LIVES CAN BE GREATLY IMPROVED BY USING THE 80/20 PRINCIPLE.
EACH INDIVIDUAL CAN BE MORE EFFECTIVE AND HAPPIER.

EACH PROFIT-SEEKING CORPORATION CAN BECOME MUCH MORE PROFITABLE.

EACH NONPROFIT ORGANIZATION CAN ALSO DELIVER MUCH MORE USEFUL OUTPUTS.

EVERY GOVERNMENT CAN ENSURE ITS CITIZENS BENEFIT MUCH MORE FROM ITS EXISTENCE.

AT THE HEART OF THIS PROGRESS IS A PROCESS OF SUBSTITUTION.
RESOURCES THAT HAVE WEAK EFFECTS IN ANY PARTICULAR USE ARE NOT USED, OR ARE USED SPARINGLY.
11
34
RESOURCES THAT HAVE POWERFUL EFFECTS ARE USED AS MUCH AS POSSIBLE.

I BELIEVE THAT THE 80/20 PRINCIPLE IS ENORMOUSLY HOPEFUL.
THERE IS A TRAGIC AMOUNT OF WASTE EVERYWHERE -- IN THE WAY NATURE OPERATES, IN BUSINESS, IN SOCIETY, AND IN OUR OWN LIVES.
IF THE TYPICAL PATTERN IS FOR 80 PERCENT OF RESULTS TO COME FROM 20 PERCENT OF INPUTS...
...IT IS NECESSARILY TYPICAL, TOO, THAT 80 PERCENT OF INPUTS HAVE ONLY MARGINAL -- 20 PERCENT -- IMPACT.
THE PARADOX IS THAT SUCH WASTE CAN BE WONDERFUL NEWS, IF WE USE THE 80/20 PRINCIPLE CREATIVELY...
...NOT JUST TO JUSTIFY AND CASTIGATE LOW PRODUCTIVITY, BUT ALSO TO DO SOMETHING POSITIVE ABOUT IT!

THERE ARE TWO ROUTES TO ACHIEVING THIS.
22
ONE IS TO REALLOCATE THE RESOURCES FROM UNPRODUCTIVE TO PRODUCTIVE USES.

THE OTHER ROUTE TO PROGRESS IS TO FIND WAYS OF MAKING THE UNPRODUCTIVE RESOURCES MORE EFFECTIVE, EVEN IN THEIR EXISTING APPLICATIONS...
...TO MAKE WEAK RESOURCES BEHAVE AS THOUGH THEY WERE THEIR MORE PRODUCTIVE COUSINS.

THE 80/20 PRINCIPLE STATES THAT THERE IS AN INBUILT IMBALANCE BETWEEN CAUSES AND RESULTS...
20
...INPUTS AND OUTPUTS...
80
...AND EFFORTS AND REWARDS.

TYPICALLY, CAUSES, INPUTS, OR EFFORT DIVIDE INTO TWO CATEGORIES.
THE MAJORITY THAT HAVE LITTLE IMPACT...

...AND A SMALL MINORITY THAT HAVE A MAJOR, DOMINANT IMPACT.

EVERY PERSON I HAVE KNOWN WHO HAS TAKEN THE 80/20 PRINCIPLE SERIOUSLY HAS EMERGED WITH USEFUL, AND, IN SOME CASES, *LIFE-CHANGING* INSIGHTS.
THERE ARE TWO WAYS TO USE THE 80/20 PRINCIPLE.
TRADITIONALLY, THE 80/20 PRINCIPLE HAS REQUIRED 80/20 ANALYSIS...
...A QUANTITATIVE METHOD TO ESTABLISH THE PRECISE RELATIONSHIP BETWEEN CAUSES/INPUTS/EFFORTS...
...AND RESULTS/OUTPUTS/REWARDS.
THIS METHOD USES THE POSSIBLE EXISTENCE OF THE 80/20 RELATIONSHIP AS A HYPOTHESIS AND THEN GATHERS THE FACTS SO THAT THE TRUE RELATIONSHIP IS REVEALED.
A NEW AND COMPLEMENTARY WAY TO USE THE 80/20 PRINCIPLE IS WHAT I CALL "80/20 THINKING."
THIS REQUIRES DEEP THOUGHT ABOUT ANY ISSUE THAT IS IMPORTANT TO YOU AND ASKS YOU TO MAKE A JUDGMENT ON WHETHER THE 80/20 PRINCIPLE IS WORKING IN THAT AREA.
LET'S LOOK FIRST AT 80/20 ANALYSIS AND THEN AT 80/20 THINKING.

80/20 ANALYSIS EXAMINES THE RELATIONSHIP BETWEEN TWO SETS OF COMPARABLE DATA.
ONE SET IS ALWAYS A UNIVERSE OF PEOPLE OR OBJECTS, USUALLY A LARGE NUMBER OF 100 OR MORE, THAT CAN BE TURNED INTO A PERCENTAGE.

THE OTHER SET OF DATA RELATES TO SOME INTERESTING CHARACTERISTIC OF THE PEOPLE OR OBJECTS THAT CAN BE MEASURED AND ALSO TURNED INTO A PERCENTAGE.

LOOK AT A GROUP OF 100 FRIENDS, ALL OF WHOM ARE AT LEAST OCCASIONAL BEER DRINKERS, AND COMPARE HOW MUCH BEER THEY DRANK LAST WEEK.

IN OUR EXAMPLE, WE ASK ALL OUR 100 FRIENDS HOW MANY GLASSES OF BEER THEY DRANK LAST WEEK AND ARRAY THE ANSWERS IN DESCENDING ORDER.

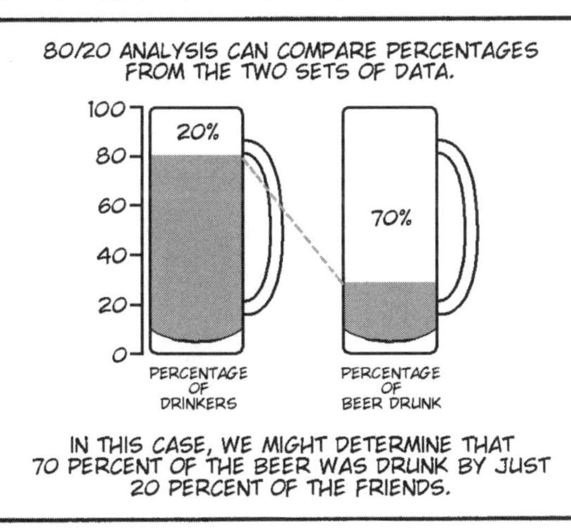
80/20 ANALYSIS CAN COMPARE PERCENTAGES FROM THE TWO SETS OF DATA.
100
80
60
40
20
0
20%
70%
PERCENTAGE OF DRINKERS
PERCENTAGE OF BEER DRUNK
IN THIS CASE, WE MIGHT DETERMINE THAT 70 PERCENT OF THE BEER WAS DRUNK BY JUST 20 PERCENT OF THE FRIENDS.

THE MOST FREQUENT OBSERVATION IS THAT 80 PERCENT OF THE QUANTITY BEING MEASURED CAME FROM 20 PERCENT OF THE PEOPLE OR OBJECTS.
80/20
20/3
80/20 HAS BECOME SHORTHAND FOR THIS TYPE OF UNBALANCED RELATIONSHIP, WHETHER OR NOT THE PRECISE RESULT IS 80/20.

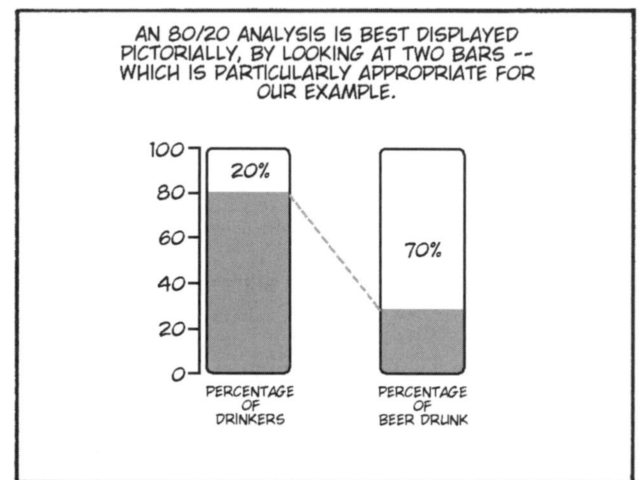
AN 80/20 ANALYSIS IS BEST DISPLAYED PICTORIALLY, BY LOOKING AT TWO BARS -- WHICH IS PARTICULARLY APPROPRIATE FOR OUR EXAMPLE.
100
80
60
40
20
0
20%
70%
PERCENTAGE OF DRINKERS
PERCENTAGE OF BEER DRUNK

80/20 ANALYSIS IS TYPICALLY USED TO CHANGE THE RELATIONSHIP IT DESCRIBES OR MAKE BETTER USE OF IT.
ONE USE IS TO CONCENTRATE ON THE KEY CAUSES OF THE RELATIONSHIP, THE 20 PERCENT OF INPUTS THAT LEAD TO THE 80 PERCENT OF OUTPUTS.
80
20

IF THE TOP 20 PERCENT OF BEER DRINKERS ACCOUNT FOR 70 PERCENT OF BEER CONSUMED, THIS IS THE GROUP THE BREWERY SHOULD CONCENTRATE ON REACHING.

NEW FREQUENT READER DISCOUNT
SIMILARLY, IF A FIRM FINDS THAT 80 PERCENT OF ITS PROFITS COME FROM 20 PERCENT OF ITS CUSTOMERS, IT SHOULD USE THIS INFORMATION TO CONCENTRATE ON KEEPING THAT 20 PERCENT HAPPY.
Line Starts Here

IF YOU ANALYZED THE ENJOYMENT YOU GET FROM YOUR LEISURE ACTIVITIES AND FOUND THAT 80 PERCENT OF THE FUN CAME FROM 20 PERCENT OF THE ACTIVITIES, IT WOULD MAKE SENSE TO INCREASE THE TIME YOU SPENT ON THE 20 PERCENT.

THE SECOND MAIN USE OF 80/20 ANALYSIS IS TO DO SOMETHING ABOUT THE "UNDERPERFORMING" 80 PERCENT OF INPUTS THAT CONTRIBUTE TO ONLY 20 PERCENT OF THE OUTPUT.

PERHAPS THE OCCASIONAL BEER DRINKER CAN BE PERSUADED TO DRINK MORE BY PROVIDING A SLIGHTLY DIFFERENT PRODUCT.
NEW! SWEET CHERRY FLAVOR!

PERHAPS YOU COULD WORK OUT WAYS TO GET GREATER ENJOYMENT OUT OF "UNDERPERFORMING" LEISURE ACTIVITIES.

WHILE 80/20 ANALYSIS IS EXTREMELY USEFUL, MOST PEOPLE ARE NOT NATURAL ANALYSTS.
THEREFORE, IF WE WANT THE 80/20 PRINCIPLE TO BE A GUIDE IN OUR DAILY LIVES, WE NEED SOMETHING LESS ANALYTICAL AND MORE INSTANTLY AVAILABLE THAN 80/20 ANALYSIS.

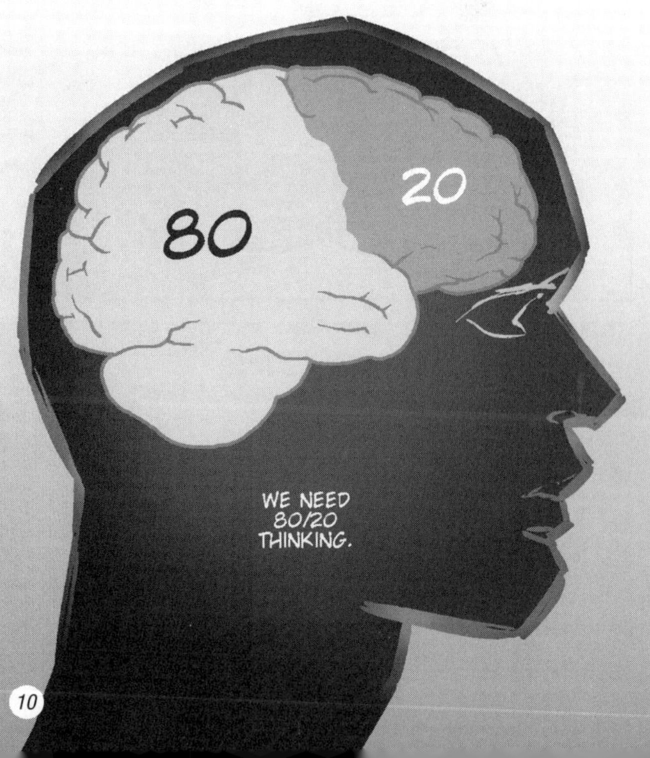
20
80
WE NEED 80/20 THINKING.

80/20 THINKING IS MY PHRASE FOR THE APPLICATION OF THE 80/20 PRINCIPLE TO DAILY LIFE.

AS WITH 80/20 ANALYSIS, WE START WITH A HYPOTHESIS ABOUT A POSSIBLE IMBALANCE BETWEEN INPUTS AND OUTPUTS.
FLOUR

BUT INSTEAD OF COLLECTING AND ANALYZING DATA, WE ESTIMATE.
80/20 THINKING REQUIRES AND ENABLES US TO SPOT THE FEW REALLY IMPORTANT THINGS WHILE IGNORING THE MASS OF UNIMPORTANT THINGS.

TO ENGAGE IN 80/20 THINKING, WE MUST CONSTANTLY ASK OURSELVES:
BAKING POWDER
Corn Starch
Stuffing
SUGAR
S
P
CAKE MIX
ROTINI
WHAT IS THE 20 PERCENT THAT LEADS TO THE 80 PERCENT?

80/20 THINKING IS THEN USED TO CHANGE BEHAVIOR TO CONCENTRATE ON THE MOST IMPORTANT 20 PERCENT.
YOU KNOW THAT 80/20 THINKING IS WORKING WHEN IT MULTIPLIES EFFECTIVENESS.

APPLICATION OF THE 80/20 PRINCIPLE IMPLIES THAT WE SHOULD CELEBRATE EXCEPTIONAL PRODUCTIVITY...
...RATHER THAN RAISE AVERAGE EFFORTS.

LOOK FOR THE SHORT CUT RATHER THAN RUN THE FULL COURSE.

EXERCISE CONTROL OVER OUR LIVES WITH THE LEAST POSSIBLE EFFORT.

BE SELECTIVE, NOT EXHAUSTIVE.

STRIVE FOR EXCELLENCE IN A FEW THINGS RATHER THAN MERELY GOOD PERFORMANCE IN MANY.

DELEGATE OR OUTSOURCE AS MUCH AS POSSIBLE IN OUR DAILY LIVES.
IN
OUT

ONLY DO THE THINGS WE ARE BEST AT DOING AND ENJOY MOST.

IN EVERY IMPORTANT SPHERE, WORK OUT WHERE 20 PERCENT OF EFFORT CAN LEAD TO 80 PERCENT OF RETURNS.
80
20

CALM DOWN, WORK LESS, AND TARGET A LIMITED NUMBER OF VERY VALUABLE GOALS WHERE THE 80/20 PRINCIPLE WILL WORK FOR US.

BECOMING AN 80/20 THINKER REQUIRES ACTIVE PARTICIPATION AND CREATIVITY ON YOUR PART.
80
20
75
25
90
10
70
30
IF YOU WANT TO BENEFIT FROM 80/20 THINKING, YOU HAVE TO DO IT!

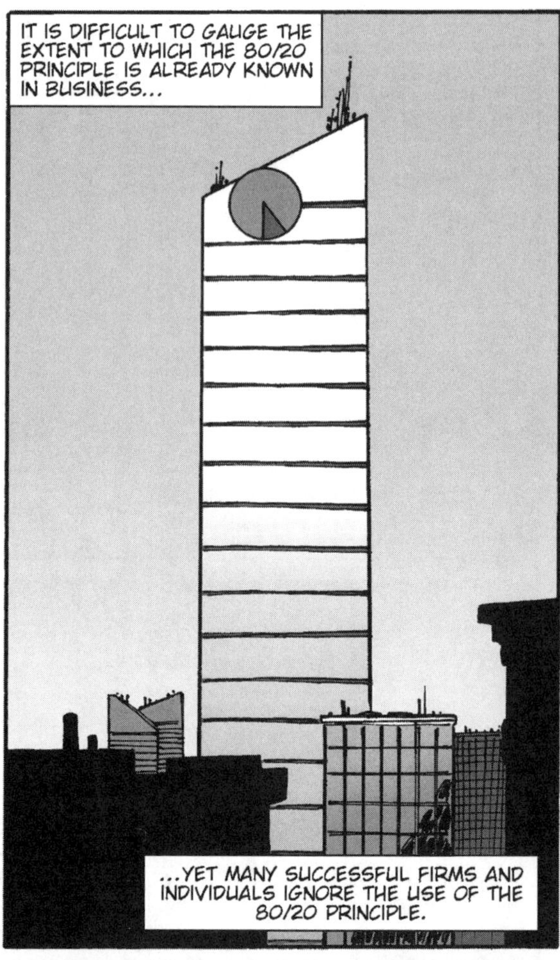
IT IS DIFFICULT TO GAUGE THE EXTENT TO WHICH THE 80/20 PRINCIPLE IS ALREADY KNOWN IN BUSINESS...
...YET MANY SUCCESSFUL FIRMS AND INDIVIDUALS IGNORE THE USE OF THE 80/20 PRINCIPLE.

80%
RESULTS
20% EFFORT
CONSIDERING THE IMPORTANCE OF THE 80/20 PRINCIPLE AND THE EXTENT TO WHICH IT IS KNOWN BY MANAGERS, IT REMAINS EXTREMELY DISCREET.

IT SOMETIMES REMAINS UNEXPLOITED, EVEN BY THOSE WHO RECOGNIZE THE IDEA.

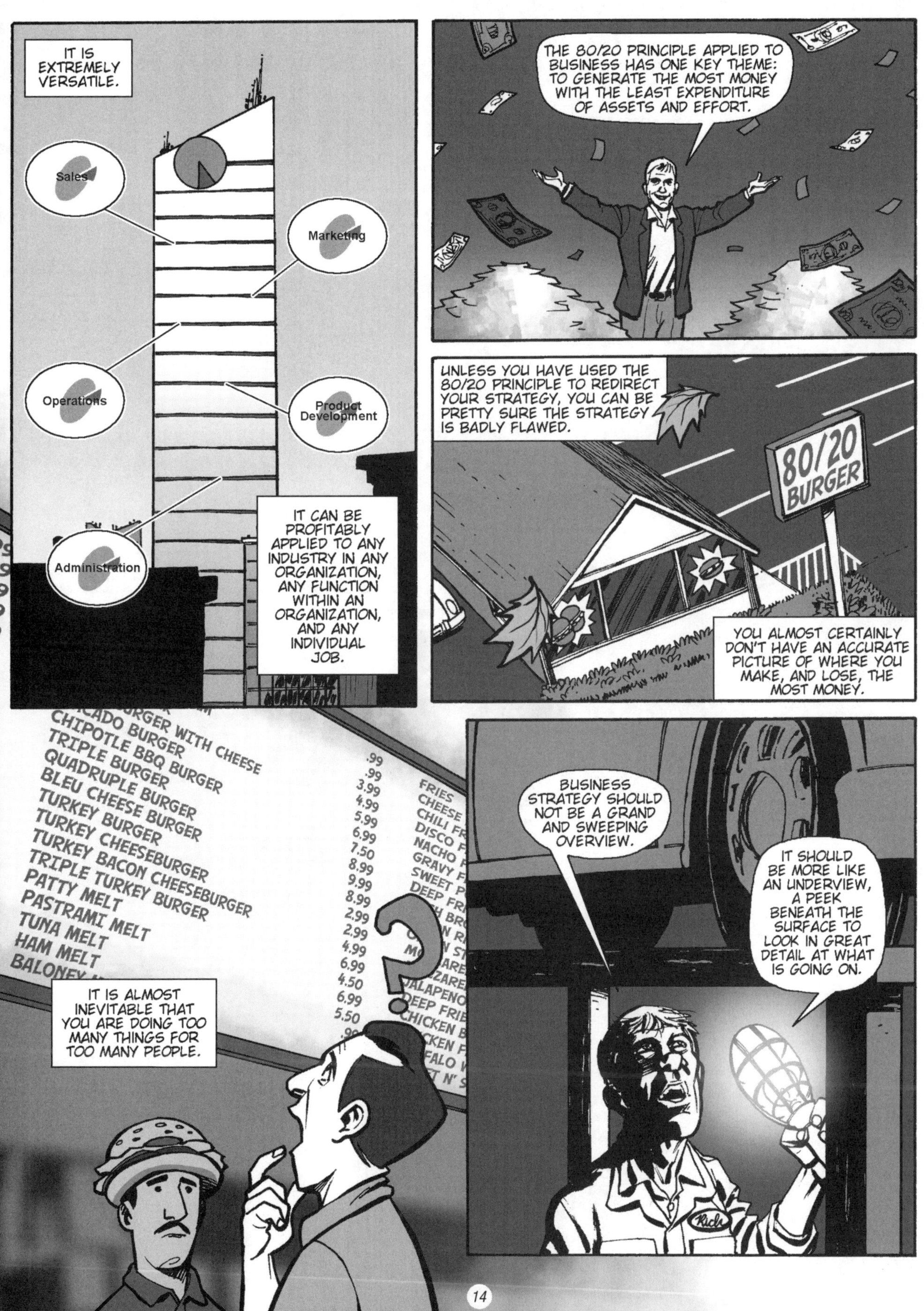

IT IS EXTREMELY VERSATILE.
Sales
Marketing
Operations
Product Development
Administration
IT CAN BE PROFITABLY APPLIED TO ANY INDUSTRY IN ANY ORGANIZATION, ANY FUNCTION WITHIN AN ORGANIZATION, AND ANY INDIVIDUAL JOB.
THE 80/20 PRINCIPLE APPLIED TO BUSINESS HAS ONE KEY THEME: TO GENERATE THE MOST MONEY WITH THE LEAST EXPENDITURE OF ASSETS AND EFFORT.
UNLESS YOU HAVE USED THE 80/20 PRINCIPLE TO REDIRECT YOUR STRATEGY, YOU CAN BE PRETTY SURE THE STRATEGY IS BADLY FLAWED.
80/20 BURGER
YOU ALMOST CERTAINLY DON'T HAVE AN ACCURATE PICTURE OF WHERE YOU MAKE, AND LOSE, THE MOST MONEY.
CHIPOTLE BBQ BURGER
TRIPLE BURGER
QUADRUPLE BURGER
BLEU CHEESE BURGER
TURKEY BURGER
TURKEY CHEESEBURGER
TURKEY BACON CHEESEBURGER
TRIPLE TURKEY BURGER
PATTY MELT
PASTRAMI MELT
TUNA MELT
HAM MELT
.99
.99
3.99
4.99
5.99
6.99
7.50
8.99
9.99
8.99
2.99
2.99
4.99
6.99
4.50
6.99
5.50
FRIES
IT IS ALMOST INEVITABLE THAT YOU ARE DOING TOO MANY THINGS FOR TOO MANY PEOPLE.
BUSINESS STRATEGY SHOULD NOT BE A GRAND AND SWEEPING OVERVIEW.
IT SHOULD BE MORE LIKE AN UNDERVIEW, A PEEK BENEATH THE SURFACE TO LOOK IN GREAT DETAIL AT WHAT IS GOING ON.
Rich

TO ARRIVE AT A USEFUL BUSINESS STRATEGY YOU NEED TO LOOK CAREFULLY AT THE DIFFERENT CHUNKS OF YOUR BUSINESS, PARTICULARLY AT THEIR PROFITABILITY AND CASH GENERATION.

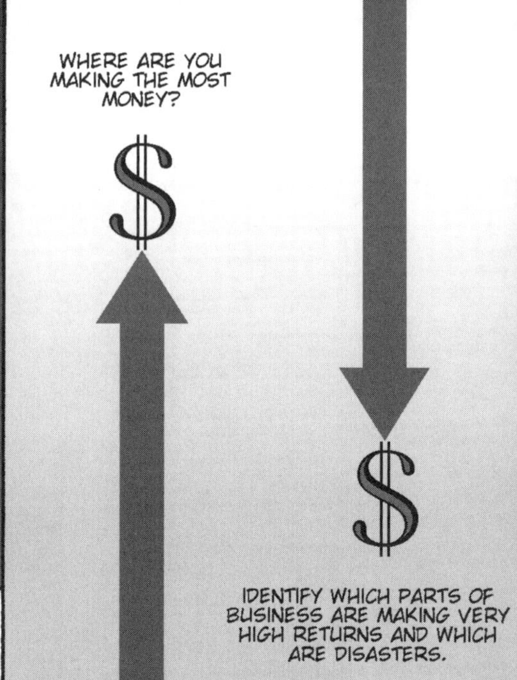
WHERE ARE YOU MAKING THE MOST MONEY?
$
$
IDENTIFY WHICH PARTS OF BUSINESS ARE MAKING VERY HIGH RETURNS AND WHICH ARE DISASTERS.

TO DO THIS WE WILL CONDUCT AN 80/20 ANALYSIS OF PROFITS BY DIFFERENT CATEGORIES OF BUSINESS:

PRODUCT OR PRODUCT GROUP/TYPE.

CUSTOMER OR CUSTOMER GROUP/TYPE.

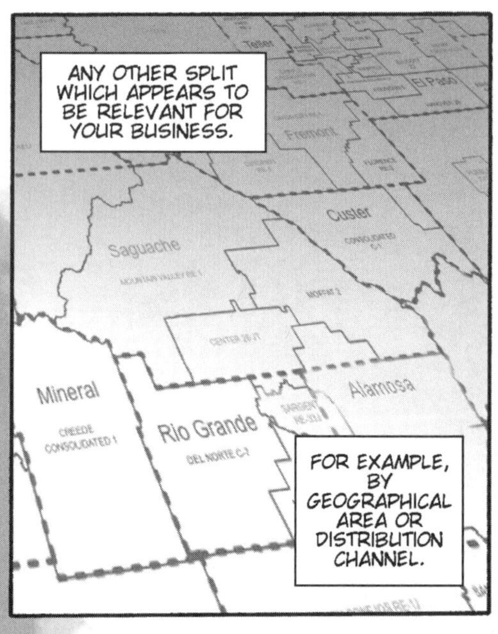
ANY OTHER SPLIT WHICH APPEARS TO BE RELEVANT FOR YOUR BUSINESS.
Fremont
Custer
Saguache
Mineral
Rio Grande
Alamosa
FOR EXAMPLE, BY GEOGRAPHICAL AREA OR DISTRIBUTION CHANNEL.

START WITH PRODUCTS.

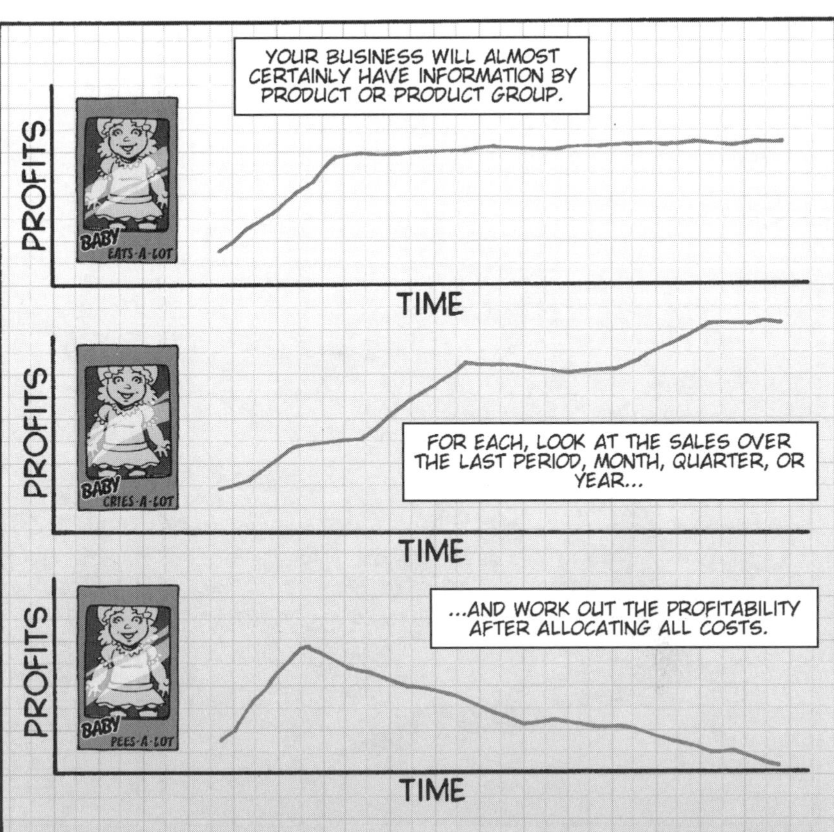
YOUR BUSINESS WILL ALMOST CERTAINLY HAVE INFORMATION BY PRODUCT OR PRODUCT GROUP.
PROFITS
BABY EATS-A-LOT
TIME
PROFITS
BABY CRIES-A-LOT
FOR EACH, LOOK AT THE SALES OVER THE LAST PERIOD, MONTH, QUARTER, OR YEAR...
TIME
PROFITS
BABY PEES-A-LOT
...AND WORK OUT THE PROFITABILITY AFTER ALLOCATING ALL COSTS.
TIME

TYPICALLY, SOME PRODUCTS, REPRESENTING A MINORITY OF TURNOVER, ARE VERY PROFITABLE.
BABY EATS-A-LOT

MOST PRODUCTS ARE MODESTLY OR MARGINALLY PROFITABLE.

AND SOME ARE REALLY MAKING LARGE LOSSES ONCE YOU ALLOCATE ALL THE COSTS.
BABY PEES-A-LOT

SOME CUSTOMERS, OFTEN SMALLER ONES, PAY HIGH PRICES BUT HAVE A HIGH COST TO SERVE.

THE VERY BIG CUSTOMERS MAY BE EASY TO DEAL WITH AND TAKE LARGE VOLUME OF THE SAME PRODUCT, BUT THEY KNOCK YOU DOWN ON PRICE.

THE BEST WAY TO EXAMINE THE PROFITABILITY OF YOUR BUSINESS IS TO BREAK IT DOWN INTO COMPETITIVE SEGMENTS.

A COMPETITIVE SEGMENT IS A PART OF YOUR BUSINESS IN WHICH YOU FACE A DIFFERENT COMPETITOR OR DIFFERENT COMPETITIVE DYNAMICS.

TAKE ANY PART OF YOUR BUSINESS THAT COMES TO MIND -- A PRODUCT, A CUSTOMER, A PRODUCT LINE SOLD TO A CUSTOMER TYPE, OR ANY OTHER SPLIT THAT MAY BE IMPORTANT TO YOU.
NOW ASK YOURSELF TWO QUESTIONS:

DO YOU FACE A DIFFERENT MAIN COMPETITOR IN THIS PART OF YOUR BUSINESS COMPARED TO THE REST OF IT?

DO YOU AND YOUR COMPETITOR HAVE THE SAME RATIO OF SALES FOR MARKET SHARE IN THE TWO AREAS, OR ARE THEY RELATIVELY STRONGER IN ONE AREA WHILE YOU'RE RELATIVELY STRONGER IN ANOTHER?
THE RULE IS SIMPLE: IF YOU DON'T FACE DIFFERENT COMPETITORS, OR DIFFERENT RELATIVE COMPETITIVE POSITIONS, IT'S NOT A SEPARATE SEGMENT.

WE TEND TO THINK THAT INNOVATION IS DIFFICULT, BUT WITH CREATIVE USE OF THE 80/20 PRINCIPLE, INNOVATION CAN BE BOTH EASY AND FUN!
CONSIDER, FOR EXAMPLE, THE FOLLOWING IDEAS:

80 PERCENT OF PROFITS MADE BY ALL INDUSTRIES ARE MADE BY ONLY 20 PERCENT OF INDUSTRIES.
MAKE A LIST OF THE MOST PROFITABLE INDUSTRIES THAT YOU ARE AWARE OF, AND ASK HOW YOUR INDUSTRY CAN BE MORE LIKE THESE.

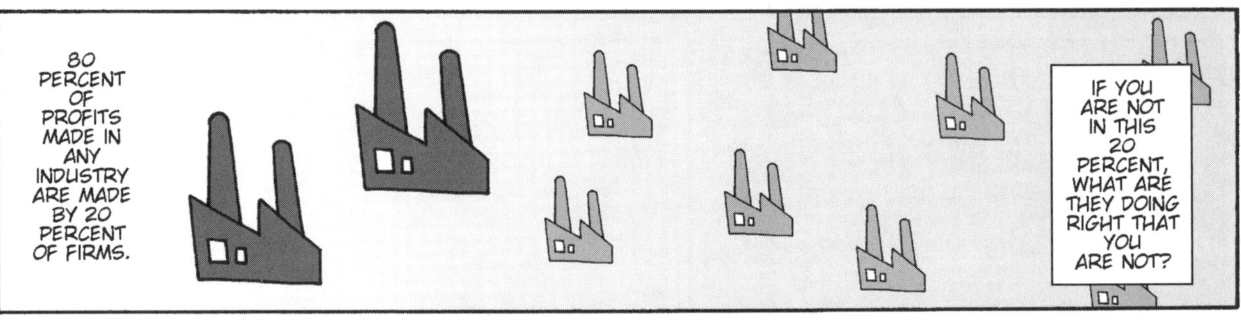
80 PERCENT OF PROFITS MADE IN ANY INDUSTRY ARE MADE BY 20 PERCENT OF FIRMS.
IF YOU ARE NOT IN THIS 20 PERCENT, WHAT ARE THEY DOING RIGHT THAT YOU ARE NOT?

80 PERCENT OF VALUE PERCEIVED BY CUSTOMERS RELATES TO 20 PERCENT OF WHAT AN ORGANIZATION DOES.
WHAT IS THAT 20 PERCENT IN YOUR CASE?
WHAT IS STOPPING YOU FROM DOING MORE OF IT?

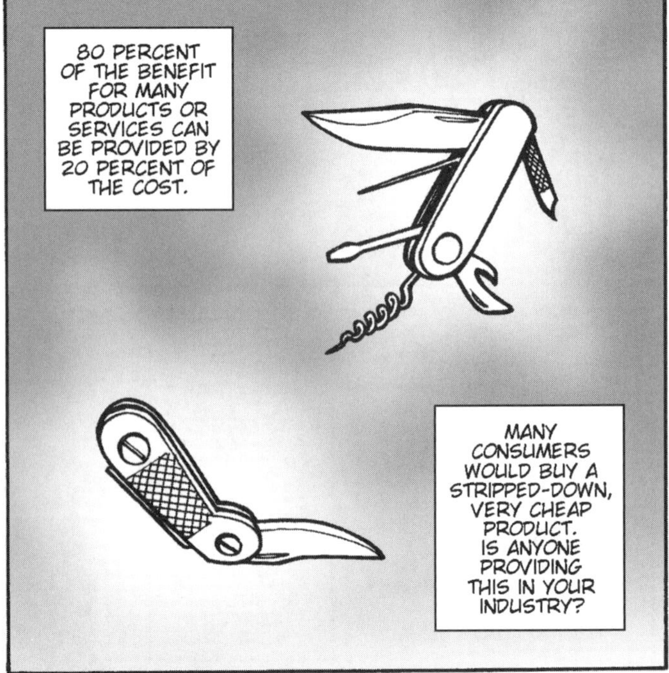
80 PERCENT OF THE BENEFIT FOR MANY PRODUCTS OR SERVICES CAN BE PROVIDED BY 20 PERCENT OF THE COST.
MANY CONSUMERS WOULD BUY A STRIPPED-DOWN, VERY CHEAP PRODUCT. IS ANYONE PROVIDING THIS IN YOUR INDUSTRY?

Stokely & Chandler
Consulting
client/stakeholder
Internal Business Process
successful strategy implementation
multi-dimensional, forward looking strategic measures
change management is the systematic management of change.
THE 80/20 PRINCIPLE SUGGESTS THAT YOUR STRATEGY IS WRONG.

IF YOU MAKE MOST OF YOUR MONEY OUT OF A SMALL PART OF YOUR ACTIVITY, YOU SHOULD TURN YOUR COMPANY UPSIDE DOWN AND CONCENTRATE YOUR EFFORTS ON MULTIPLYING THE SMALL PART.
YET THIS IS ONLY PART OF THE ANSWER. BEHIND THE NEED FOR FOCUS LURKS AN EVEN MORE POWERFUL TRUTH ABOUT BUSINESS.

THOSE OF US WHO BELIEVE IN THE 80/20 PRINCIPLE WILL NEVER SUCCEED IN TRANSFORMING INDUSTRY UNTIL WE CAN DEMONSTRATE THAT SIMPLE IS BEAUTIFUL.

UNLESS PEOPLE UNDERSTAND THIS, THEY WILL NEVER BE WILLING TO GIVE UP 80% OF THEIR CURRENT BUSINESS AND OVERHEAD.

THE FIRST 75 YEARS OF THE 20TH CENTURY WITNESSED A PROGRESSIVE AND UNSTOPPABLE EXPANSION IN THE SIZE OF INDUSTRIAL ENTERPRISE...
...AND, HISTORICALLY, IN THE PORTION OF BUSINESS ACTIVITY TAKEN BY THE LARGEST FIRMS.

LEMONADE
25¢
RECENTLY, THOUGH, THE LATTER TREND HAS REVERSED.

WHY IS IT THAT LARGER FIRMS ARE LOSING MARKET SHARE TO SMALLER FIRMS?
LEMONADE
AND WHY ARE THE ADVANTAGES OF SCALE AND MARKET SHARE NOW FAILING TO TRANSLATE INTO HIGHER PROFITABILITY?

WHY IS IT THAT FIRMS OFTEN SEE THEIR SALES MUSHROOM -- YET THE RETURNS ON SALES AND CAPITAL ACTUALLY FALL RATHER THAN RISE?
PROFITS

THE MOST IMPORTANT ANSWER IS THE COST OF COMPLEXITY.
THE PROBLEM IS NOT EXTRA SCALE -- IT'S EXTRA COMPLEXITY.

LEMONADE
25¢
LEMONADE
25¢
LEMONADE
25¢
25¢
ADDITIONAL SCALE WITHOUT ADDITIONAL COMPLEXITY WILL ALWAYS GIVE LOWER UNIT COSTS.

DELIVERING TO ONE CUSTOMER MORE OF ONE PRODUCT OR SERVICE, PROVIDED THAT IT IS EXACTLY THE SAME, WILL ALWAYS RAISE RETURNS.

YET ADDITIONAL SCALE IS RARELY JUST MORE OF THE SAME.
EMONADE
MENU
LEMONADE .50
STRAWBERRY .75
APPLE
GRAPE
LIMEADE .50
KIWI .90
XTRA SUGAR
MELONADE
CITRUSADE
BLUEBERRY
CELERY
EVEN IF THE CUSTOMER IS THE SAME, THE EXTRA VOLUME USUALLY COMES FROM ADAPTING AN EXISTING PRODUCT, PROVIDING A NEW PRODUCT, OR ADDING MORE SERVICE.

THIS REQUIRES EXPENSIVE OVERHEAD COSTS THAT ARE OFTEN HIDDEN.
AND INTERNAL COMPLEXITY HAS HUGE HIDDEN COSTS.

WHEN NEW BUSINESS IS DIFFERENT FROM EXISTING BUSINESS, EVEN IF IT IS ONLY *SLIGHTLY* DIFFERENT, COSTS TEND TO GO UP.

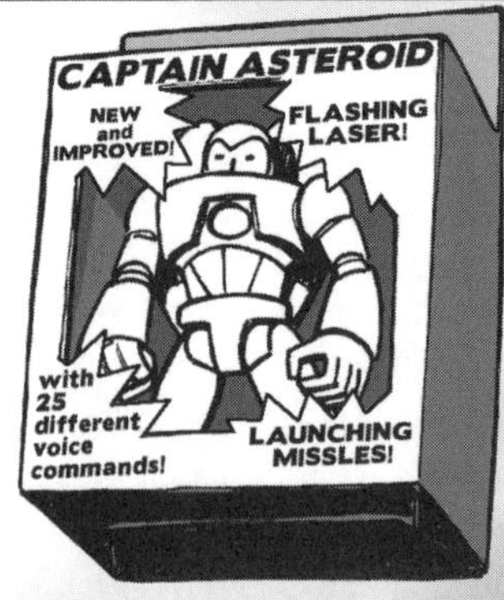

THIS IS BECAUSE COMPLEXITY SLOWS DOWN SIMPLE SYSTEMS AND REQUIRES THE INTERVENTION OF MANAGERS TO DEAL WITH THE NEW REQUIREMENTS.

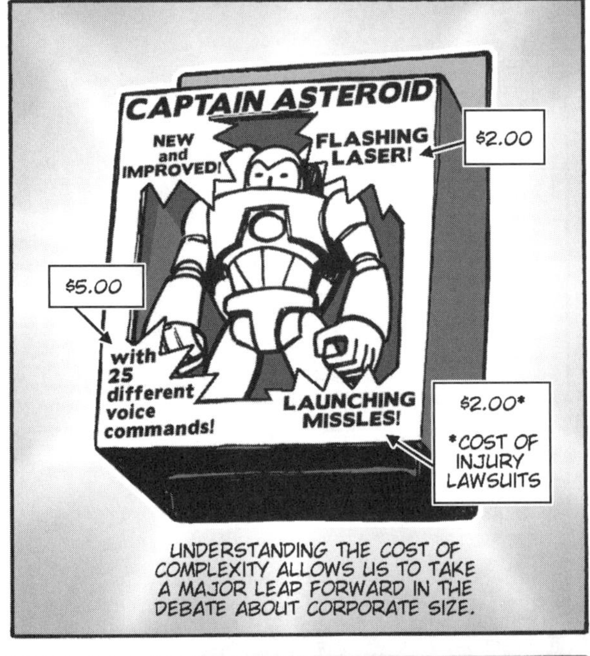

FREQUENTLY, MANAGERS FACED WITH THE RESULTS OF AN 80/20 ANALYSIS PROTEST THAT THEY CANNOT JUST FOCUS ON THE MOST PROFITABLE SEGMENTS.
THEY POINT OUT THAT THE LESS PROFITABLE SEGMENTS, AND EVEN THE LOSS-MAKING SEGMENTS, MAKE A POSITIVE CONTRIBUTION TO OVERHEADS.

THIS IS ONE OF THE LAMEST AND MOST SELF-SERVING DEFENSE MECHANISMS EVER CONTRIVED.

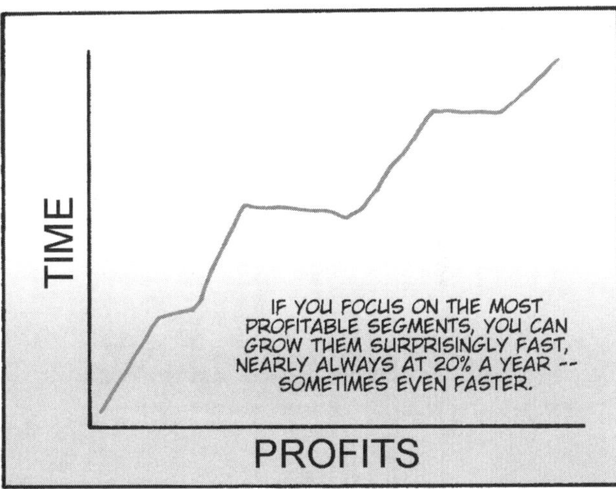
TIME
PROFITS
IF YOU FOCUS ON THE MOST PROFITABLE SEGMENTS, YOU CAN GROW THEM SURPRISINGLY FAST, NEARLY ALWAYS AT 20% A YEAR -- SOMETIMES EVEN FASTER.

WHAT IS SIMPLEST AND STANDARDIZED IS FAR MORE PRODUCTIVE AND COST-EFFECTIVE THAN WHAT IS TOO COMPLEX.

THE SIMPLEST MEASURES ARE THE MOST APPEALING AND UNIVERSAL TO COLLEAGUES, CONSUMERS, AND SUPPLIERS.
K.I.S.S.
THE SIMPLEST STRUCTURES AND PROCESS FLOWS ARE AT ONCE THE MOST ATTRACTIVE AND THE MOST COST-EFFECTIVE.

IDENTIFY THE SIMPLEST 20 PERCENT OF ANY PRODUCT RANGE,
PROCESS,
MARKETING MESSAGE,
SALES CHANNEL,
PRODUCT DESIGN,
PRODUCT MANUFACTURER,
SERVICE DELIVERY,
AND CUSTOMER FEEDBACK MECHANISM.
20
20

CULTIVATE THE SIMPLEST 20 PERCENT.
REFINE IT UNTIL IT IS AS SIMPLE AS YOU CAN MAKE IT.

MAKE THE SIMPLEST 20 PERCENT AS HIGH QUALITY AND CONSISTENT AS IMAGINABLE.
20

THE ROAD TO HELL IS PAVED WITH THE PURSUIT OF VOLUME.
VOLUME LEADS TO MARGINAL PRODUCTS, MARGINAL CUSTOMERS, AND GREATLY INCREASED MANAGERIAL COMPLEXITY.

WHY DO THE SUPPOSEDLY PROFIT MAXIMIZING ORGANIZATIONS BECOME COMPLEX WHEN IT CLEARLY DESTROYS VALUE?

ALAS, MANAGERS LOVE COMPLEXITY.
COMPLEXITY IS STIMULATING AND INTELLECTUALLY CHALLENGING. IT CREATES INTERESTING JOBS FOR MANAGERS.

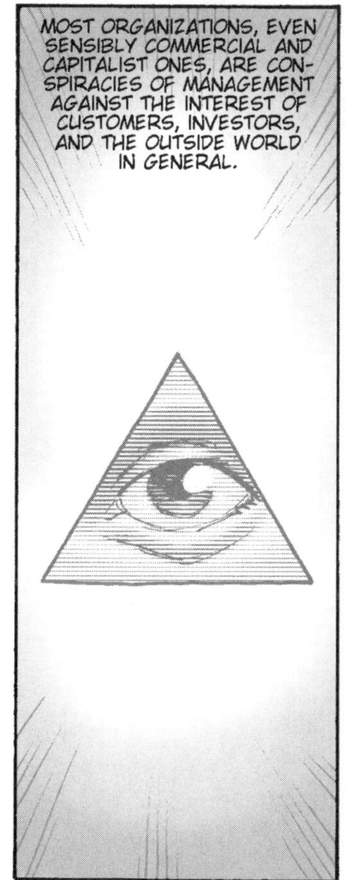
MOST ORGANIZATIONS, EVEN SENSIBLY COMMERCIAL AND CAPITALIST ONES, ARE CONSPIRACIES OF MANAGEMENT AGAINST THE INTEREST OF CUSTOMERS, INVESTORS, AND THE OUTSIDE WORLD IN GENERAL.

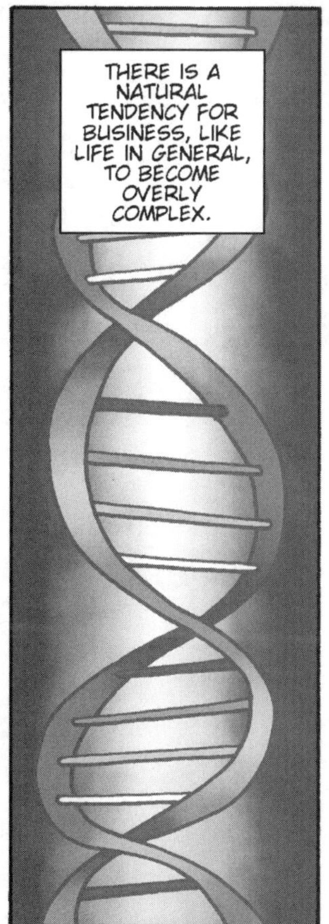
THERE IS A NATURAL TENDENCY FOR BUSINESS, LIKE LIFE IN GENERAL, TO BECOME OVERLY COMPLEX.

ALL ORGANIZATIONS, ESPECIALLY LARGE AND COMPLEX ONES, ARE INHERENTLY INEFFICIENT AND WASTEFUL.
THEY DO NOT FOCUS ON WHAT THEY SHOULD BE DOING.

WASTE THRIVES ON COMPLEXITY. EFFECTIVENESS REQUIRES *SIMPLICITY.*

THE MASS OF ACTIVITY WILL ALWAYS BE POINTLESS, POORLY CONCEIVED, BADLY DIRECTED, WASTEFULLY EXECUTED, AND LARGELY BESIDE THE POINT TO CUSTOMERS.
I'M WITH STUPID
STUPID'S WITH ME

A SMALL PORTION OF ACTIVITY WILL ALWAYS BE TERRIFICALLY EFFECTIVE AND VALUED BY CUSTOMERS.

POOR PERFORMANCE IS ALWAYS ENDEMIC, HIDING BEHIND AND SUCCORED BY A SMALLER AMOUNT OF EXCELLENT PERFORMANCE.

ALL ORGANIZATIONS ARE A MIX OF PRODUCTIVE AND UNPRODUCTIVE FORCES, INCLUDING PEOPLE, RELATIONSHIPS, AND ASSETS.

IF YOU STUDY THE OUTPUT YOUR FIRM GENERATES, CHANCES ARE THAT A QUARTER TO A FIFTH OF THE ACTIVITY ACCOUNTS FOR THREE QUARTERS OR 4/5 OF PROFITS.
MULTIPLY THAT QUARTER OR FIFTH. MULTIPLY THE EFFECTIVENESS OF THE REST -- OR CUT IT OUT.

ALL EFFECTIVE TECHNIQUES TO REDUCE COST USE THREE 80/20 INSIGHTS.

TODAY'S POINTLESS MEETING CANCELLED
SIMPLIFICATION THROUGH ELIMINATION OF UNPROFITABLE ACTIVITY.

SALES
OPERATIONS
MARKETING
FOCUS ON A FEW KEY DRIVERS OF IMPROVEMENTS.

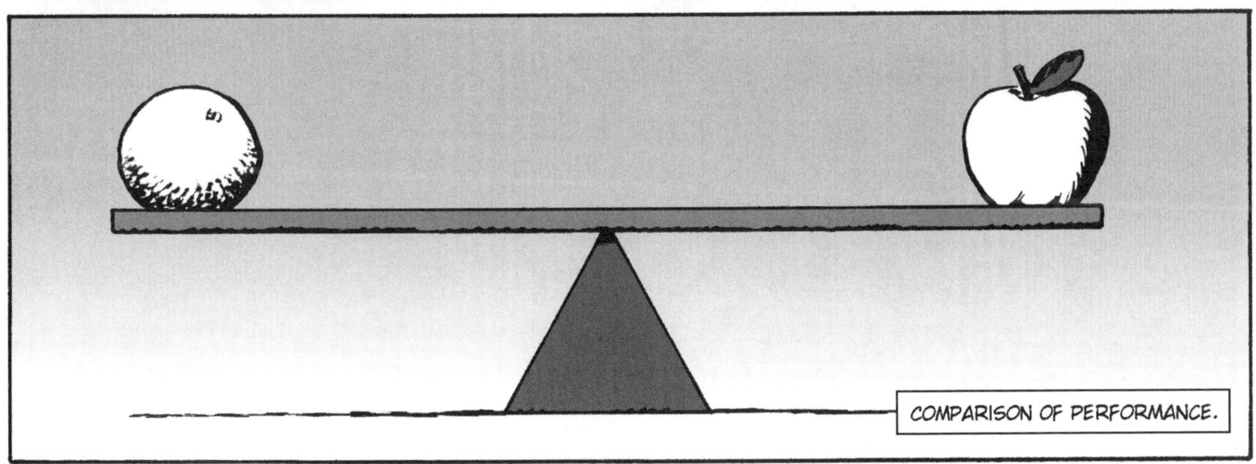
COMPARISON OF PERFORMANCE.

DO NOT TACKLE EVERYTHING WITH EQUAL EFFORT.
WALL

COST REDUCTION IS AN EXPENSIVE BUSINESS!
IDENTIFY THE AREAS (PERHAPS ONLY 20 PERCENT OF THE WHOLE BUSINESS) THAT HAVE THE GREATEST COST-REDUCTION POTENTIAL.

CONCENTRATE 80 PERCENT OF YOUR EFFORTS HERE.

80/20 ANALYSIS CAN ESTABLISH WHY PARTICULAR PROBLEMS ARISE AND FOCUS ATTENTION ON THE KEY AREAS OF IMPROVEMENT.

LET'S IMAGINE THAT YOU ARE RUNNING A BOOK PUBLISHING FIRM, AND YOUR TYPESETTING COSTS ARE 30 PERCENT OVER BUDGET.

YOUR PRODUCT MANAGER TELLS YOU THAT THERE ARE 1,001 REASONS FOR THE OVERRUN.

SOMETIMES THE AUTHORS ARE LATE WITH THE MANUSCRIPT.
SOMETIMES THE PROOFREADERS OR INDEX COMPILERS TAKE LONGER THAN PLANNED.
THE BOOK IS LONGER THAN PLANNED.

ONE THING YOU CAN DO IS TAKE A PARTICULAR TIME PERIOD, SAY THREE MONTHS, TO CAREFULLY MONITOR THE CAUSES OF ALL THE TYPESETTING COST OVERRUNS.

IF THE MAJOR CAUSES ALL RELATE TO AUTHORS, THE PUBLISHING HOUSE COULD SOLVE THE PROBLEM BY WRITING A CLAUSE INTO THE AUTHORS' CONTRACTS...
CONTRAC
...MAKING THEM LIABLE FOR ANY EXTRA TYPESETTING COSTS CAUSED BY THEIR BEING LATE OR MAKING TOO MANY LAST-MINUTE CORRECTIONS.

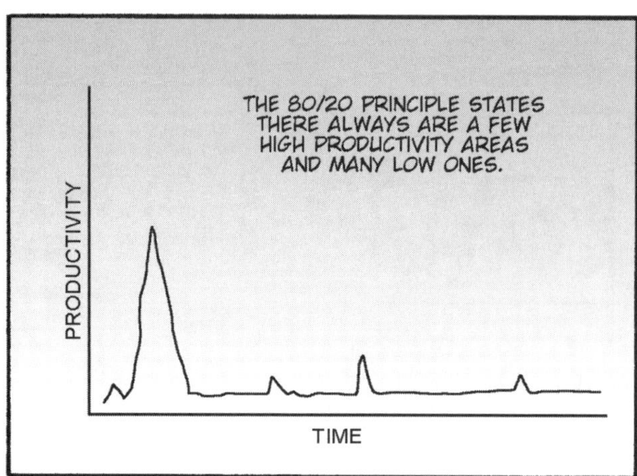
THE 80/20 PRINCIPLE STATES THERE ALWAYS ARE A FEW HIGH PRODUCTIVITY AREAS AND MANY LOW ONES.
PRODUCTIVITY
TIME

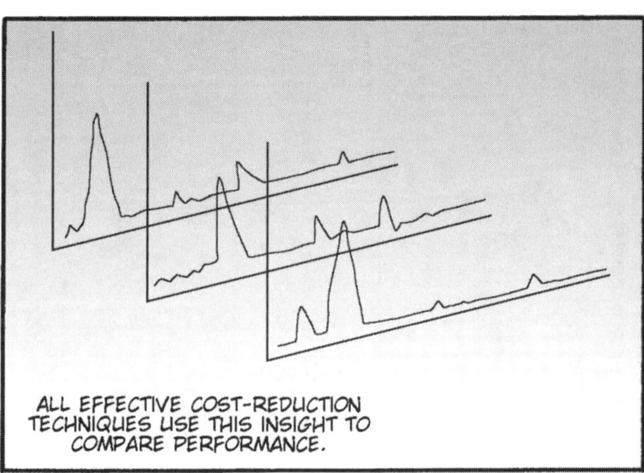
ALL EFFECTIVE COST-REDUCTION TECHNIQUES USE THIS INSIGHT TO COMPARE PERFORMANCE.

THE ONUS IS PLACED ON THE MAJORITY OF LAGGARDS TO IMPROVE PERFORMANCE TO THE LEVEL OF THE BEST...
HAPPY RETIREMENT, BILL!
...OR TO RETIRE GRACEFULLY FROM THE FIELD.

BECAUSE BUSINESS IS WASTEFUL, AND BECAUSE COMPLEXITY AND WASTE FEED ON EACH OTHER, A SIMPLE BUSINESS WILL ALWAYS BE BETTER THAN A COMPLEX ONE.
80/20 THINKING REQUIRES AND ENABLES US TO SPOT THE FEW REALLY IMPORTANT THINGS THAT ARE HAPPENING WHILE IGNORING THE MASS OF UNIMPORTANT ONES.

BECAUSE SCALE IS NORMALLY VALUABLE, IT IS BETTER TO HAVE A LARGER BUSINESS.
THE LARGE AND SIMPLE BUSINESS IS BEST.

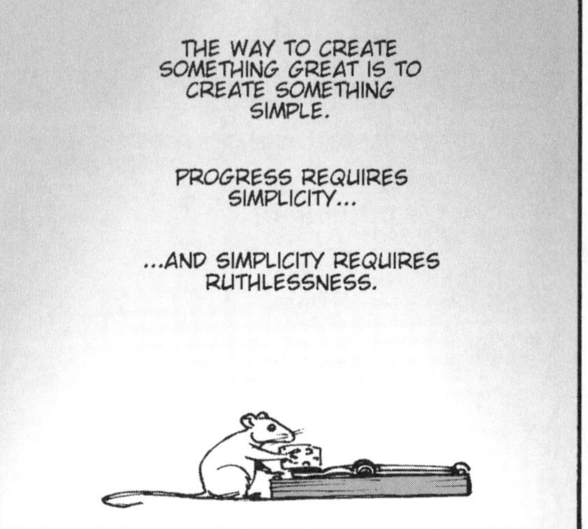
THE WAY TO CREATE SOMETHING GREAT IS TO CREATE SOMETHING SIMPLE.
PROGRESS REQUIRES SIMPLICITY...
...AND SIMPLICITY REQUIRES RUTHLESSNESS.

THE 80/20 PRINCIPLE IS ESSENTIAL FOR DOING THE RIGHT KIND OF SELLING AND MARKETING AND FOR RELATING THIS TO ANY ORGANIZATION'S OVERALL STRATEGY...
...INCLUDING THE WHOLE PROCESS OF PRODUCING AND DELIVERING GOODS AND SERVICES.

THE MARKETS AND CUSTOMERS ON WHICH ANY FIRM SHOULD BE CENTERED MUST BE THE RIGHT ONES...
...TYPICALLY A SMALL MINORITY OF THOSE THE COMPANY CURRENTLY OWNS.

MARKETING, AND THE WHOLE FIRM, SHOULD FOCUS ON PROVIDING A STUNNING PRODUCT AND SERVICE IN 20 PERCENT OF THE EXISTING PRODUCT LINE.
THE SMALL PART THAT GENERATES 80 PERCENT OF FULLY COSTED PROFITS.

NEW!
EXTRAORDINARY ENDEAVOR MUST BE DEVOTED TO FINDING, KEEPING, AND EXPANDING SALES TO THE 20 PERCENT OF CUSTOMERS WHO PROVIDE 80 PERCENT OF THE FIRM'S SALES AND PROFITS.

THERE IS NO REAL CONFLICT BETWEEN PRODUCTION AND MARKETING.
EXCLUSIVE TO OUR LOCATION
YOU WILL ONLY BE SUCCESSFUL IN MARKETING IF WHAT YOU ARE MARKETING IS DIFFERENT AND, FOR YOUR TARGET CUSTOMERS, EITHER UNOBTAINABLE ELSEWHERE...
...OR PROVIDED BY YOU AT A PRODUCT PACKAGE THAT IS A MUCH BETTER VALUE THAN IS OBTAINABLE ELSEWHERE.

SALES IS MARKETING'S CLOSE COUSIN: THE FRONT-LINE ACTIVITY TO COMMUNICATE WITH AND, AT LEAST AS IMPORTANT, TO ***LISTEN*** TO CUSTOMERS.
80/20 THINKING, AS YOU WILL SEE, IS JUST AS CRUCIAL FOR SALES AS IT IS FOR MARKETING.

THE KEY TO SUPERIOR SALES PERFORMANCE IS TO STOP THINKING AVERAGES AND START THINKING 80/20.
TAKE ANY SALESFORCE AND PERFORM AN 80/20 ANALYSIS.

IT IS ODDS ON THAT YOU'LL FIND AN UNBALANCED RELATIONSHIP BETWEEN SALES AND SALESPEOPLE.
MOST STUDIES FIND THAT THE TOP 20 PERCENT OF SALESPEOPLE GENERATE BETWEEN 70 AND 80 PERCENT OF SALES.

THERE ARE TWO SETS OF REASONS WHY SALES PER SALESPERSON VARIES SO MUCH.
THE FIRST SET RELATES TO PURE SALES FORCE PERFORMANCE ISSUES.

THE SECOND RELATES TO STRUCTURAL ISSUES OF CUSTOMER FOCUS.

SUPPOSE YOU FIND THAT 20 PERCENT OF YOUR SALES PERSONNEL ARE GENERATING 70 PERCENT OF YOUR SALES.
WHAT SHOULD YOU DO ABOUT IT?

ONE OBVIOUS, BUT OFTEN NEGLECTED, IMPERATIVE IS TO HANG ONTO THE HIGH PERFORMERS.
BONU$

NEXT, HIRE MORE OF THE SAME TYPE OF SALESPERSON.

THIRD, TRY TO IDENTIFY WHEN THE TOP SALESPEOPLE SELL THE MOST AND WHAT THEY DID DIFFERENTLY.

FOURTH, GET EVERYONE TO ADOPT THE METHODS THAT HAVE THE HIGHEST RATIO OF OUTPUT TO INPUT.

FIFTH, SWITCH A SUCCESSFUL TEAM FROM ONE AREA WITH AN UNSUCCESSFUL TEAM FROM ANOTHER AREA.

SALES TRAINING
FINALLY, CONSIDER SALES FORCE TRAINING.

ONLY TRAIN THOSE YOU ARE REASONABLY SURE PLAN TO STICK AROUND WITH YOU FOR SEVERAL YEARS.
GET YOUR BEST SALESPEOPLE TO TRAIN THEM, REWARDING THE SALES SUPERSTARS ACCORDING TO THE SUBSEQUENT PERFORMANCE OF THEIR TRAINEES.

WELCOME TO SALES TRAINING
INVEST THE MOST IN THOSE WHO PERFORM BEST AFTER THE FIRST SERIES OF TRAINING.

CHANNEL MARKETING AND SALES EFFORTS WHERE YOU CAN OFFER A MINORITY OF POTENTIAL CUSTOMERS SOMETHING UNIQUE OR OF A BETTER VALUE THAN THEY CAN OBTAIN ELSEWHERE.
BEST IN CLASS
BEST PRODUCT
CRITIC'S CHOICE

BUSINESS REQUIRES DECISIONS.

FREQUENT, FAST, AND OFTEN WITHOUT MUCH IDEA WHETHER THEY'RE RIGHT OR WRONG.

THERE ARE FIVE RULES OF DECISION MAKING WITH THE 80/20 PRINCIPLE.

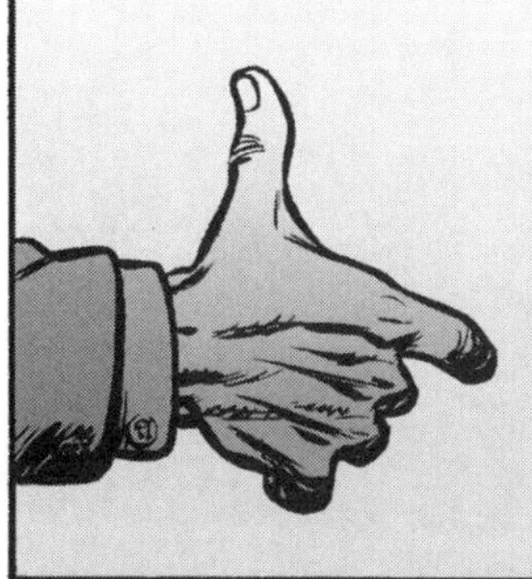

THE *THIRD RULE* OF DECISION MAKING IS FOR IMPORTANT DECISIONS: GATHER 80 PERCENT OF THE DATA AND PERFORM 80 PERCENT OF THE RELEVANT ANALYSIS IN THE FIRST 20 PERCENT OF TIME AVAILABLE.

THEN MAKE A DECISION 100 PERCENT OF THE TIME -- AND ACT DECISIVELY AS IF YOU ARE 100 PERCENT CONFIDENT THAT DECISION IS RIGHT.

FOURTH, IF WHAT YOU HAVE DECIDED ISN'T WORKING, CHANGE YOUR MIND EARLY RATHER THAN LATE.

THE ART OF PROJECT MANAGEMENT IS TO FOCUS ALL TEAM MEMBERS ON THE FEW THINGS THAT REALLY MATTER.
SIMPLIFY THE OBJECTIVE.

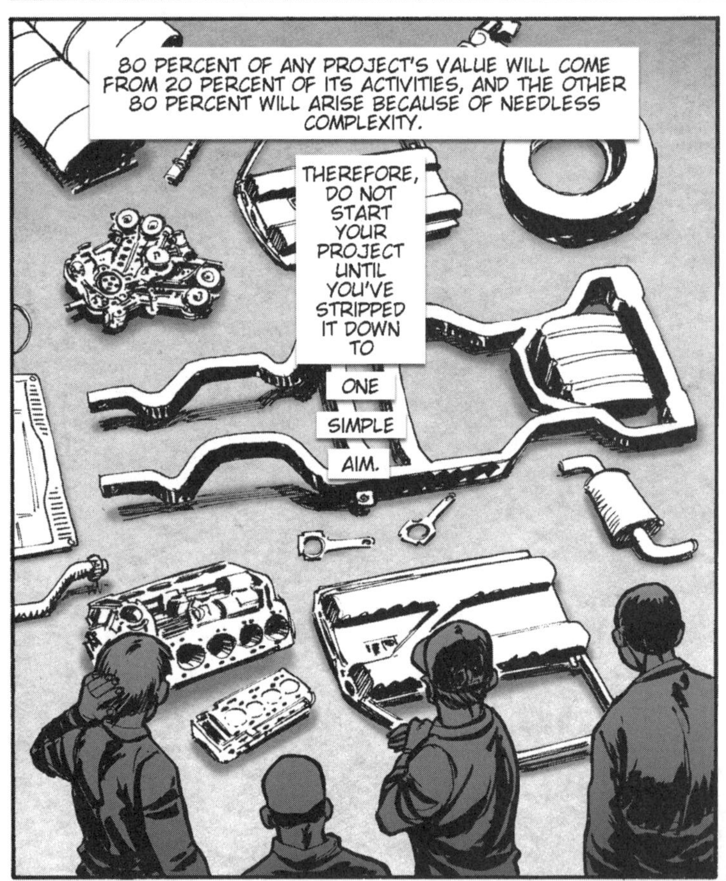
80 PERCENT OF ANY PROJECT'S VALUE WILL COME FROM 20 PERCENT OF ITS ACTIVITIES, AND THE OTHER 80 PERCENT WILL ARISE BECAUSE OF NEEDLESS COMPLEXITY.
THEREFORE, DO NOT START YOUR PROJECT UNTIL YOU'VE STRIPPED IT DOWN TO
ONE
SIMPLE
AIM.

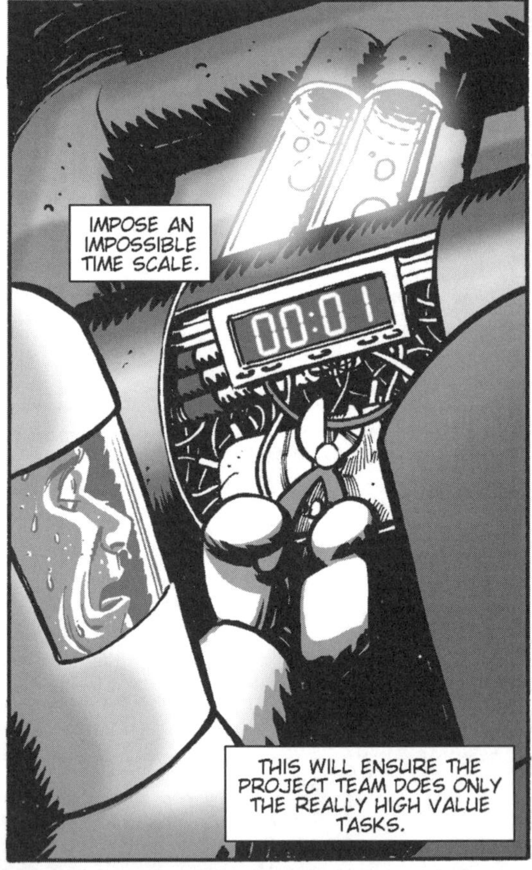
IMPOSE AN IMPOSSIBLE TIME SCALE.
00:01
THIS WILL ENSURE THE PROJECT TEAM DOES ONLY THE REALLY HIGH VALUE TASKS.

PLAN BEFORE YOU ACT.
THE SHORTER THE TIME ALLOWED FOR A PROJECT, THE GREATER PROPORTION OF TIME SHOULD BE ALLOWED FOR ITS DETAILED PLANNING AND THINKING THROUGH.

IN THE PLANNING PHASE, WRITE DOWN ALL THE CRITICAL ISSUES YOU ARE TRYING TO RESOLVE.

0 1 2 3 4 5 6 7 8 9 10

IF THERE ARE MORE THAN SEVEN OF THESE, BUMP OFF THE LEAST IMPORTANT.

THE 80/20 PRINCIPLE COMPRISES RADAR AND AUTOPILOT.
THE RADAR GIVES YOU INSIGHT TO SPOT OPPORTUNITIES AND DANGERS.

THE AUTOPILOT ALLOWS YOU TO STROLL AROUND THE BUSINESS ARENA AND TALK TO CUSTOMERS WHO MIGHT MATTER, KNOWING THAT YOU'RE STILL IN CONTROL OF YOUR DESTINY.

THE LOGIC OF THE 80/20 PRINCIPLE REQUIRES US TO GRASP AND INTERNALIZE A FEW SIMPLE POINTS.

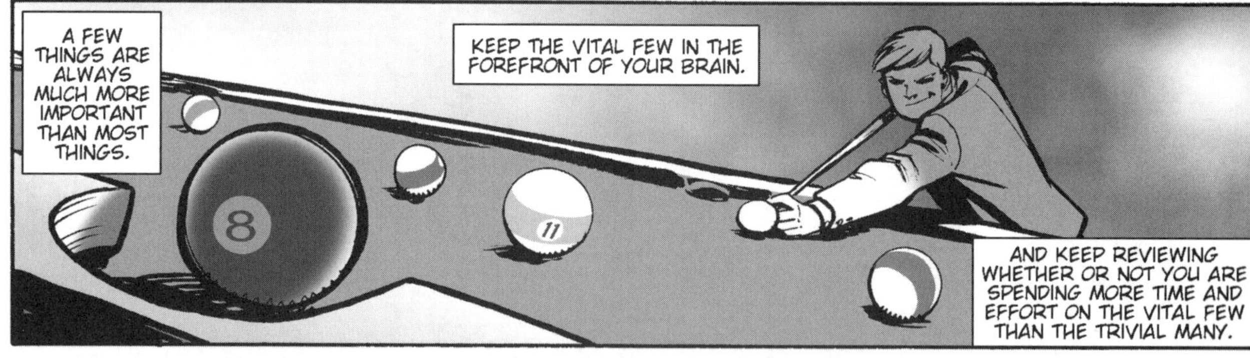
A FEW THINGS ARE ALWAYS MUCH MORE IMPORTANT THAN MOST THINGS.
KEEP THE VITAL FEW IN THE FOREFRONT OF YOUR BRAIN.
8
11
AND KEEP REVIEWING WHETHER OR NOT YOU ARE SPENDING MORE TIME AND EFFORT ON THE VITAL FEW THAN THE TRIVIAL MANY.

PROGRESS MEANS MOVING RESOURCES FROM LOW-VALUE TO HIGH-VALUE USES.

RESOURCES ARE ALWAYS MISALLOCATED.

SUCCESS IS UNDERRATED AND UNDER RECOGNIZED.
OFTEN IT IS DISMISSED AS A LUCKY STREAK.
80

EQUILIBRIUM IS ILLUSORY. NOTHING LASTS FOREVER, AND NOTHING IS EVER IN EQUILIBRIUM.
INNOVATION IS THE ONLY CONSTANT. IT IS ALWAYS RESISTED BUT RARELY EXTINGUISHED.

CHANGE IS NECESSARY FOR SURVIVAL.
CONSTRUCTIVE CHANGE REQUIRES INSIGHT INTO WHAT IS MOST EFFECTIVE AND A FOCUS ON THAT WINNING WAY.

THE BIGGEST WINS ALL START SMALL.
SOMETHING BIG ALWAYS COMES FROM SOMETHING SMALL:
SMALL CAUSES
SMALL PRODUCTS
SMALL FIRMS
SMALL MARKETS
SMALL SYSTEMS.

THE 80/20 PRINCIPLE, LIKE THE TRUTH, CAN SET YOU FREE.
YOU CAN WORK LESS, BUT AT THE SAME TIME, EARN AND ENJOY MORE.

THE ONLY PRICE IS THAT YOU NEED TO DO SOME SERIOUS 80/20 THINKING.
THIS WILL YIELD A FEW KEY INSIGHTS THAT, IF YOU ACT ON THEM, COULD CHANGE YOUR LIFE.

THE OBJECTIVE OF 80/20 THINKING IS TO GENERATE ACTION THAT WILL MAKE SHARP IMPROVEMENTS IN YOUR LIFE.
ACTION OF THE TYPE DESIRED REQUIRES UNUSUAL INSIGHT. INSIGHT REQUIRES REFLECTION AND INTROSPECTION.

INSIGHT SOMETIMES REQUIRES DATA GATHERING, AND WE WILL INDULGE GENTLY IN A LITTLE OF THIS AS IT RELATES TO YOUR OWN LIFE.

OUR OBJECTIVE AS 80/20 THINKERS IS TO LEAVE ACTION BEHIND, DO SOME QUIET THINKING, MINE A FEW SMALL PIECES OF PRECIOUS INSIGHT...
...AND THEN ACT, SELECTIVELY, ON A FEW OBJECTIVES IN THE NARROW FRONT.

80/20 THINKING IS UNCONVENTIONAL.
IT IS CONVENTIONAL WISDOM THAT LEADS TO WASTE IN THE FIRST PLACE.

THE POWER OF THE 80/20 PRINCIPLE LIES IN DOING THINGS DIFFERENTLY BASED ON UNCONVENTIONAL WISDOM.
THIS REQUIRES YOU TO WORK OUT WHY MOST OTHER PEOPLE ARE DOING THINGS WRONG OR TO A FRACTION OF THEIR POTENTIAL.
IF YOUR INSIGHTS ARE NOT UNCONVENTIONAL, YOU ARE NOT THINKING 80/20.

80/20 THINKING IS HEDONISTIC.
80/20 THINKING SEEKS PLEASURE. IT BELIEVES LIFE IS MEANT TO BE ENJOYED.
IT BELIEVES THAT MOST ACHIEVEMENT IS A BYPRODUCT OF INTEREST, JOY, AND THE DESIRE FOR FUTURE HAPPINESS.

80/20 THINKING BELIEVES IN PROGRESS.
80/20 THINKING IS INHERENTLY OPTIMISTIC BECAUSE, PARADOXICALLY, IT REVEALS A STATE OF AFFAIRS THAT IS SERIOUSLY BELOW WHAT IT *SHOULD* BE.

80/20 THINKING IS STRATEGIC.
80/20 THINKING IS NONLINEAR.
LINEAR THINKING IS ATTRACTIVE BECAUSE IT IS SIMPLE, CUT AND DRY.
THE TROUBLE IS THAT IT IS A POOR DESCRIPTION OF THE WORLD -- AND AN EVEN WORSE PREPARATION FOR CHANGING IT.

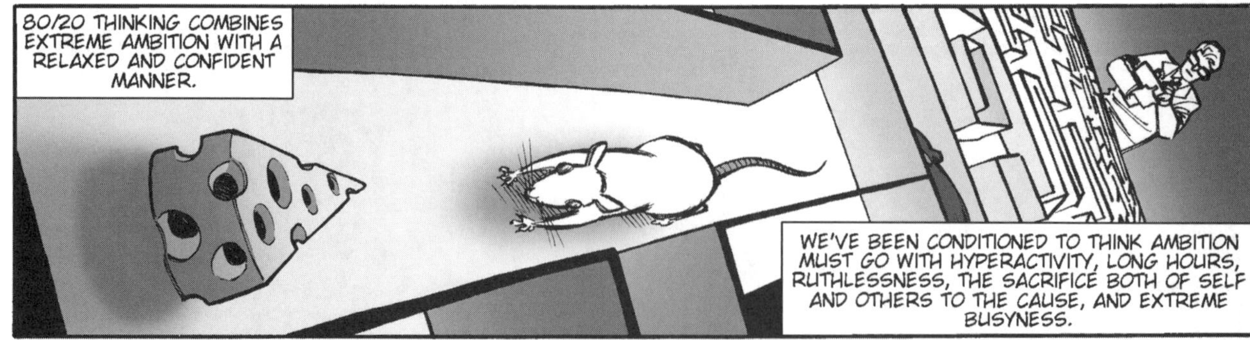
80/20 THINKING COMBINES EXTREME AMBITION WITH A RELAXED AND CONFIDENT MANNER.
WE'VE BEEN CONDITIONED TO THINK AMBITION MUST GO WITH HYPERACTIVITY, LONG HOURS, RUTHLESSNESS, THE SACRIFICE BOTH OF SELF AND OTHERS TO THE CAUSE, AND EXTREME BUSYNESS.

A MUCH MORE ATTRACTIVE COMBINATION IS THAT OF EXTREME AMBITION WITH CONFIDENCE, RELAXATION, AND A CIVILIZED MANNER.
THIS IS THE 80/20 IDEA, BUT IT RESTS ON SOLID FOUNDATIONS.

MOST GREAT ACHIEVEMENTS ARE MADE THROUGH A COMBINATION OF STEADY APPLICATION AND SUDDEN INSIGHT.
THINK OF NEWTON SITTING UNDER A TREE BEING STRUCK BY AN APPLE.
bip

ALMOST EVERYONE NEEDS A TIME REVOLUTION.
THE 80/20 PRINCIPLE, WHEN APPLIED TO OUR USE OF TIME, ADVANCES THE FOLLOWING HYPOTHESIS...
12

MOST OF ANY INDIVIDUAL'S SIGNIFICANT ACHIEVEMENTS ARE ACHIEVED IN A MINORITY OF THEIR TIME.

SIMILARLY, MOST OF AN INDIVIDUAL'S HAPPINESS OCCURS DURING QUITE BOUNDED PERIODS OF TIME.

WORK OUT WHAT YOU WANT FROM LIFE.
MOST OF US DON'T WORK OUT WHAT WE WANT -- AND END UP WITH LOPSIDED LIVES AS A RESULT.

REMEMBER THE PROMISE OF THE 80/20 PRINCIPLE.
IF WE TAKE NOTE OF WHAT IT TELLS US, WE CAN WORK LESS, EARN MORE, ENJOY MORE, AND ACHIEVE MORE.

TO DO THIS, WE MUST START WITH A ROUNDED VIEW OF EVERYTHING WE WANT.
START WITH ***LIFESTYLE.***

DO YOU ENJOY YOUR LIFE?
AND WHETHER YOU DO OR NOT, IS THERE A LIFESTYLE THAT COULD SUIT YOU BETTER?

AM I LIVING WITH THE RIGHT PERSON?
AM I LIVING IN THE RIGHT PLACE?
AM I WORKING THE RIGHT HOURS?
DOES MY LIFESTYLE MAKE IT EASY FOR ME TO BE CREATIVE AND FULFILL MY POTENTIAL?

WHAT ABOUT **WORK?**
WORK IS A KEY PART OF LIFE, BUT ALMOST NO ONE SHOULD ALLOW WORK TO TAKE OVER THEIR LIVES, HOWEVER MUCH THEY CLAIM TO ENJOY IT.

IF ON AVERAGE YOU ARE HAPPIER OUTSIDE WORK, YOU SHOULD WORK LESS AND/OR CHANGE YOUR JOB.

WHAT ABOUT **MONEY?**
MOST PEOPLE HAVE PECULIAR VIEWS ABOUT MONEY. THEY THINK IT'S MORE IMPORTANT THAN IT IS -- AND THAT IT'S MORE DIFFICULT TO GET THAN IT IS.
MTA

HOW DO YOU OBTAIN MONEY IN THE FIRST PLACE?
THE BEST ANSWER, ONE THAT WORKS SURPRISINGLY OFTEN, IS TO DO SOMETHING YOU ENJOY.

MONEY IS **OVERRATED.**
IT'D BE GREAT TO HAVE A LOT MORE MONEY, BUT DON'T GO OVERBOARD.
REMEMBER THAT THE MORE MONEY YOU HAVE, THE LESS VALUE AN EXTRA DOLLOP OF WEALTH CREATES.

WHAT ABOUT ***ACHIEVEMENT?***
ACHIEVEMENT SHOULD BE ***EASY.***

IT SHOULDN'T BE "99 PERCENT PERSPIRATION AND ONE PERCENT INSPIRATION."
INSTEAD, SEE IF IT'S TRUE THAT 80 PERCENT OF YOUR ACHIEVEMENT TO DATE HAS COME FROM 20 PERCENT OF YOUR INPUTS.
IF TRUE OR NEARLY TRUE, THINK CAREFULLY ABOUT THIS TOP 20 PERCENT.

RIP
WITHOUT RELATIONSHIPS, WE ARE EITHER DEAD TO THE WORLD --
OR JUST DEAD.

OUR FRIENDSHIPS ARE AT THE HEART OF OUR LIVES.

IT IS ALSO TRUE THAT OUR PROFESSIONAL RELATIONSHIPS ARE AT THE HEART OF OUR SUCCESS.
WHAT ON EARTH HAS THIS GOT TO DO WITH THE 80/20 PRINCIPLE?

WE DEVOTE MUCH LESS THAN 80 PERCENT OF OUR ATTENTION TO THE 20 PERCENT OF RELATIONSHIPS THAT CREATE 80 PERCENT OF THE VALUE.

25
5.0
YOU MAY NEED TO HAVE MORE THAN ONE RUN AT THE NUMBERS TO MAKE THEM ADD UP TO 100 BY THE TIME YOU'RE FINISHED.

14:34:15
40
COMPLETE THIS EXERCISE BY NOTING AGAINST EACH NAME THE PROPORTION OF TIME YOU ACTIVELY SPEND WITH THE PERSON.

6.0
4.5
0.2
THE ACTION IMPLICATIONS SHOULD BE PLAIN.
9.0
0.5
40
GO FOR QUALITY RATHER THAN QUANTITY.

SPEND YOUR TIME AND EMOTIONAL ENERGY REINFORCING AND DEEPENING THE RELATIONSHIPS THAT ARE MOST IMPORTANT.

NOW TURN TO YOUR RELATIONSHIPS AND ALLIANCES RELATED TO YOUR WORK.

HERE THE IMPORTANCE OF A FEW CLOSE ALLIES CAN HARDLY BE OVERSTATED.

YOU ALONE CANNOT MAKE YOURSELF SUCCESSFUL.
Employee of the Month
NOMINATIONS
ONLY OTHERS CAN DO THAT FOR YOU.

WHAT YOU *CAN* DO IS SELECT THE BEST RELATIONSHIPS AND ALLIANCES FOR YOUR PURPOSES.

YOU BADLY NEED FRIENDS AND ALLIES.
YOU MUST TREAT THEM WELL, EVEN AS AN EXTENSION OF YOURSELF.

NOTHING IS MORE IMPORTANT THAN YOUR CHOICE OF ALLIANCES.
WITHOUT THEM YOU ARE NOTHING.
WITH THEM YOU CAN TRANSFORM YOUR LIFE -- AND OFTEN THE LIVES OF THOSE AROUND YOU.

ONE 80/20 HYPOTHESIS WOULD BE THAT 80% OF HAPPINESS OCCURS IN 20 PERCENT OF OUR TIME.

HERE ARE TWO WAYS TO BE HAPPIER!

IDENTIFY THE TIMES WHEN YOU ARE HAPPIEST, AND EXPAND ON THEM AS MUCH AS POSSIBLE.

80-20 LAWN CARE
IDENTIFY THE TIMES WHEN YOU ARE LEAST HAPPY, AND REDUCE THEM AS MUCH AS POSSIBLE.

EQ
WE CAN ALSO MAKE OURSELVES HAPPY BY STRENGTHENING OUR EMOTIONAL INTELLIGENCE.

EMOTIONAL INTELLIGENCE INCLUDES ABILITIES SUCH AS BEING ABLE TO MOTIVATE ONESELF AND DELAY GRATIFICATION...
...TO REGULATE ONE'S MOODS AND TO KEEP STRESS FROM STOPPING THE ABILITY TO THINK, TO EMPATHIZE, AND TO HOPE.

THE GOOD NEWS IS THAT EMOTIONAL INTELLIGENCE CAN BE CULTIVATED AND LEARNED.

WE CAN MAKE OURSELVES HAPPIER BY CHANGING THE WAY WE THINK ABOUT EVENTS.

WE ALL HAVE EXPERIENCED THE TRAP OF SELF-REINFORCED DEPRESSION.

WHEN WE THINK IN A GLOOMY OR NEGATIVE WAY, WE SIMPLY MAKE THINGS WORSE.

OPTIMISM, IT SEEMS, IS A MEDICALLY APPROVED INGREDIENT FOR BOTH SUCCESS AND HAPPINESS -- AND THE GREATEST MOTIVATOR ON EARTH.

WE CAN MAKE OURSELVES HAPPIER BY CHANGING THE WAY WE THINK ABOUT EVENTS.

DO YOU THINK OF YOURSELF AS SUCCESSFUL OR UNSUCCESSFUL?
IF YOU OPT FOR UNSUCCESSFUL, YOU CAN BE SURE THERE ARE MANY PEOPLE WHO ACHIEVE LESS THAN YOU HAVE AND WOULD BE DESCRIBED BY MOST AS LESS SUCCESSFUL THAN YOU ARE.

YOUR PERCEPTION OF SELF-SUCCESS CONTRIBUTES BOTH TO YOUR SUCCESS AND TO YOUR HAPPINESS.

WE CAN MAKE OURSELVES HAPPIER BY CHANGING EVENTS.

A FURTHER ROUTE TO SUPERIOR HAPPINESS IS TO CHANGE THE EVENTS YOU ENCOUNTER IN ORDER TO INCREASE YOUR HAPPINESS.
MISS 80-20
NONE OF US CAN EVER HAVE COMPLETE CONTROL OVER EVENTS, BUT WE CAN HAVE MUCH MORE CONTROL THAN WE THINK.

IF THE BEST WAY TO START BEING HAPPY IS TO STOP BEING UNHAPPY...
MISS 80-20
...THE FIRST THING WE SHOULD DO IS AVOID SITUATIONS AND PEOPLE THAT TEND TO MAKE US DEPRESSED.

AFTER YOU HAVE REMOVED-- OR SET IN MOTION PLANS TO REMOVE-- THE CAUSES OF UNHAPPINESS, CONCENTRATE ENERGY ON THE POSITIVE SEEKING OF HAPPINESS.

HAPPINESS IS A DUTY. WE SHOULD CHOOSE TO BE HAPPY. WE SHOULD WORK TO HAPPINESS.

DOS SANTOS
80-20
IN DOING SO, WE SHOULD HELP THOSE CLOSEST TO US, AND EVEN THOSE WHO JUST STUMBLED ACROSS US, SHARE OUR HAPPINESS.

WHAT WE ALL NEED IS A SET OF DAILY HAPPINESS HABITS, SIMILAR TO OUR DAILY FITNESS OR HEALTHY EATING REGIMES.

THERE ARE SEVEN DAILY HAPPINESS HABITS!

EXERCISE.

MENTAL STIMULATION.

SPIRITUAL/ARTISTIC STIMULATION/MEDITATION.

DOING A GOOD TURN.

TAKING A PLEASURE BREAK WITH A FRIEND.

GIVING YOURSELF A TREAT.

pat pat pat
CONGRATULATING YOURSELF.

REALIZE THAT THE FUTURE IS ALREADY HERE.

REMEMBER THE 80/20 PRINCIPLE.
PROGRESS ALWAYS COMES FROM A SMALL MINORITY OF PEOPLE AND ORGANIZED RESOURCES WHO DEMONSTRATE THAT PREVIOUSLY ACCEPTED CEILINGS OR PERFORMANCE CAN BECOME FLOORS FOR EVERYONE.

PROGRESS REQUIRES ELITES, BUT ELITES WHO LIVE FOR GLORY AND SERVICE TO SOCIETY -- WHO ARE WILLING TO PLACE THEIR GIFTS AT THE DISPOSAL OF US ALL.

PROGRESS DEPENDS ON INFORMATION ABOUT EXCEPTIONAL ACHIEVEMENT AND THE DIFFUSION OF SUCCESSFUL EXPERIMENTS...

...ON BREAKING DOWN THE STRUCTURES ERECTED BY THE MASS OF VESTED INTERESTS...

VOTING BOOTH
...ON DEMANDING THAT THE STANDARDS ENJOYED BY A PRIVILEGED MINORITY SHOULD BE AVAILABLE TO ALL.

YOU CAN START PRACTICING IN YOUR PROFESSIONAL AND PERSONAL LIFE **NOW.**

YOU CAN ISOLATE THE PARTS OF YOUR CHARACTER, WORK, LIFESTYLE, AND RELATIONSHIPS THAT, MEASURED AGAINST THE TIME AND ENERGY INVOLVED, GIVE YOU VALUE GREATER THAN THE DAILY GRIND.

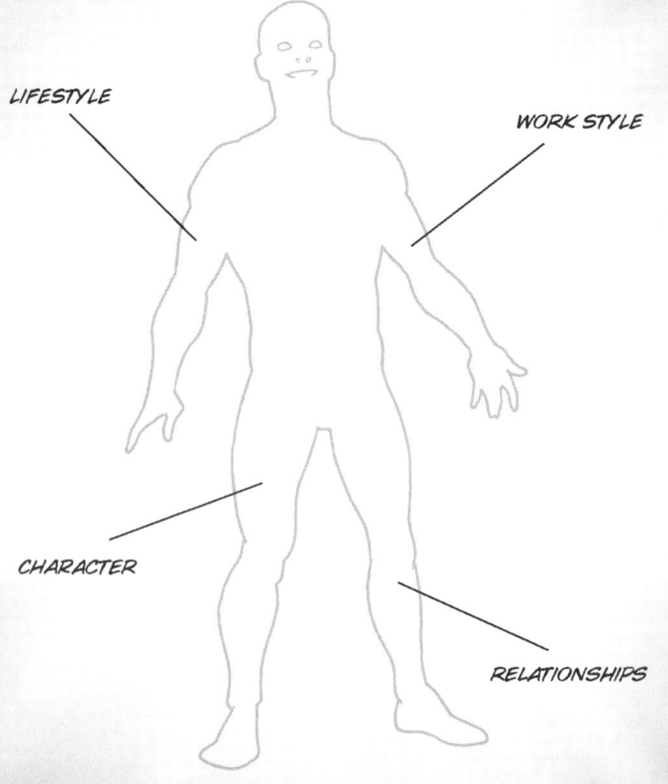

YOU CAN TAKE YOUR OWN SMALL FRAGMENTS OF GREATEST ACHIEVEMENT, HAPPINESS, AND SERVICE TO OTHERS, AND MAKE THEM A MUCH LARGER PART OF YOUR LIFE.

WITH THE 80/20 PRINCIPLE, YOU CAN BECOME A BETTER, MORE USEFUL, AND ***HAPPIER*** HUMAN BEING!

About the Author

Richard Koch has made a huge fortune, many times his original investment, from the companies he has started, turned around, or helped expand dramatically: these include Filofax, Belgo Restaurants, Plymouth Gin, and Betfair (Europe‘s largest and most profitable Internet gambling business).

Koch graduated from Oxford University and received an MBA from the Wharton School of University of Pennsylvania.

He was formerly a consultant with Boston Consulting Group and a partner of Bain & Company.

A self-confessed „lazy entrepreneur“, he lives the 80/20 way in Gibraltar, Cape Town, and the sunniest parts of Spain and Portugal.

About the Artist

Nobody has a better understanding of the 80-20 principle than a comics artist -- to toil for hours and hours every day for about a month, drawing tiny pictures in little boxes -- the final product being a 6 x 10 inch pamphlet that you can read in less than 15 minutes.

Chris Moreno has been doing this for 10 years.

Well, he hasn't just been drawing comics this whole time, for companies such as Marvel, idw, boom! studios, and image -- not to mention his own creator-owned comics, like Sanz Pantz: Ninja platypus, Dysfunctianimals, super frat, and the new zombie dickheads. he's also spent long stretches of time and effort creating art for roleplaying and video games for Kenzer & Co. and 2k games, not to mention book illustration, storyboards and concepts for film, tv, and advertising. Countless days, weeks and months spent creating artwork that goes into the creation of the quickly consumed entertainment that you enjoy every day.

but you won't hear him complain. nope! because from that 80 percent of effort that goes towards 20 percent of the results, he gets 100 percent satisfaction from doing it. and isn't that what it's all about?

if you'd like to see more of how chris spends his time, you can check out these sites:

www.chrismoreno.org

chrismoreno.deviantart.com

www.superfrat.com

dysfunctianimals.blogspot.com

Other titles from SmarterComics™

SHUT UP, STOP WHINING & GET A LIFE from SmarterComics

by Larry Winget

Internationally renowned success philosopher, business speaker, and humorist, Larry Winget offers advice that flies in the face of conventional self-help. SHUT UP, STOP WHINING, AND GET A LIFE forces all responsibility for every aspect of your life right where it belongs: on you.

THE ART OF WAR from SmarterComics

by Sun Tzu

Written by an ancient Chinese military general and philosopher, THE ART OF WAR reveals the subtle secrets of successful competition – equally applicable to war, business, politics, sports, law, poker, gaming, and life. Required reading in modern business schools!

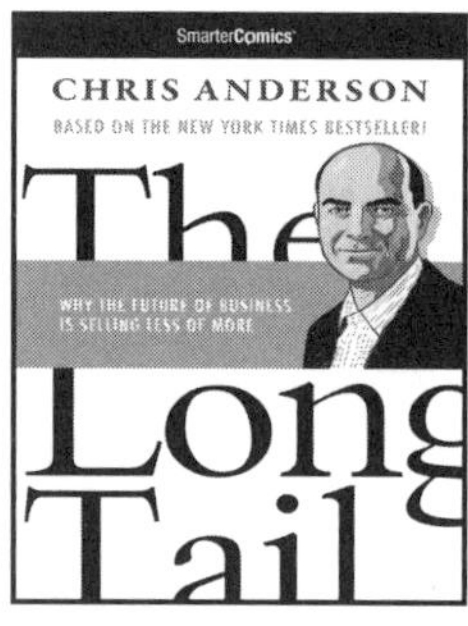

THE LONG TAIL from SmarterComics

by Chris Anderson

Now in comic format, this 2006 New York Times bestseller introduced the business world to a future that's already here. It explains why the focus of Internet commerce is not on hits but on misses-the long tail of the demand curve – and illuminates the reasons behind the success of niche operations like Amazon.com, iTunes, and Netflix. A must-read for every entrepreneur

OVERACHIEVEMENT from SmarterComics

by Dr. John Eliot

In OVERACHIEVEMENT from SmarterComics, Dr. Eliot offers the rest of us the unconventional and counterintuitive concepts embraced by Olympic athletes, business moguls, rock stars, top surgeons, salespeople, and financial experts who have turned to him for performance-enhancement advice.

Other titles from SmarterComics™

HOW TO MASTER THE ART OF SELLING from SmarterComics

by Tom Hopkins

A national bestseller, with over one million copies sold in its original version, this book is a classic for teaching the tools of selling success. Lauded by motivational icon Zig Ziglar, the author has been called "America's #1 sales trainer."

FORTUNE FAVORS THE BOLD from SmarterComics

by Franco Arda

Written by the founder of SmarterComics, this powerful little manual packs a punch. If you want to grab life by the horns but tend to drag your feet doing it, this comic is for you.

THINK & GROW RICH from SmarterComics

by Napoleon Hill

Want to learn the principles of getting rich in less than an hour? Take the illustrated advice of millionaire Andrew Carnegie, whose observations make up the heart of the best-selling classic "Think and Grow Rich." Now updated into an engaging comic book format, you can quickly glean Carnegie's wisdom from these beautifully illustrated panels.

THE BOOK OF 5 RINGS from SmarterComics

by Miyamoto Musashi

Infamous 17th century samurai Miyamoto Musashi (1584-1645) never lost a fight. His unprecedented winning streak wasn't based on supernatural powers: he was a keen master of strategy, timing, and the nuances of human interaction. He recorded his brilliant observations in „The Book of Five Rings“ in 1643.

QUIZ

Please visit www.smartercomics.com/quiz for the answers and more quizzes.

Q: The 80/20 Principle can:

A. Help individuals and groups achieve more with much less effort.

B. Raise personal effectiveness and happiness.

C. All of the above.

Q: The 80/20 Principle asserts that:

A. The harder you work on the most important 80% of a project, the more successful you will be.

B. 20% of causes, inputs, or effort usually lead to 80% of results, outputs, or rewards.

C. 80% of causes, inputs, or effort typically yield 20% of results, outputs, or rewards.

Q: The pattern underlying the 80/20 Principle:

A. It has been recognized by businesses for centuries.

B. Was only discovered in the last 25 years.

C. Was discovered in 1897 by Italian economist Vilfredo Pareto.

Q: "80/20 Thinking" is used to describe:

A. The application of the 80/20 Principle to daily life.

B. The in-depth analysis that should go into every project.

C. An inability to execute a project due to over-thinking.

Q: Why is it that firms often see their sales mushroom yet the returns on sales and capital actually fall, rather than rise as the theory would predict?

A. They have set prices too low.

B. They have spent too much on marketing.

C. The cost of complexity.

Q: When it comes to corporate size:

A. Small is best.

B. Large is best.

C. Large and simple is best.

Q: You should not start a new team project until:

A. All members of the team are in agreement on the direction of the project.

B. You have all budgets for the project allotted.

C. You have stripped the project down to one simple aim.

Q: If our friendships are the heart of our lives, our professional relationships are:

A. The heart of our 9 – 5 day.

B. The heart of our success.

C. Unimportant when compared to family and friends.

Q: Aristotle said that the goal of all human activity should be:

A. Happiness.

B. Wealth.

C. The recognition of peers.

Q: Conventional wisdom leads to:

A. Success in all endeavors.

B. Rapid change.

C. Waste.

SmarterComics
20
80
By Richard Koch
Based on the international bestseller

www.smartercomics.com